Meet Me at the Door

LIBRARY OF CONGRESS CATALOG CARD NUMBER: 71-85044

ERNEST GORDON

Meet Me at the Door

 HARPER & ROW, PUBLISHERS
New York, Evanston, and London

1817

Meet Me at the Door

to Helen

1

THE TELEPHONE bell violated impudently the privacy of the night. I was startled into unexpected consciousness. Where am I? What is it? I thought anxiously. I picked up the telephone next to my bed.

"I've got to see you. I've got to see you," said a voice in answer to my groggy hello.

"Where?" I heard myself saying.

"In your study, right away, please come."

By this time I was conscious enough to turn on a lamp and look at my wristwatch. It was 3:15 A.M., 3:15 of a Sunday morning. Drat. I needed my sleep. The voice was urgent, demanding, frightened. It could not be a practical joke. It had to be sincere.

"Okay, okay. Meet me at the door opposite the sundial." The telephone at the other end clicked into silence.

Helen was now awake and concerned. "What's up? What's that?"

"Oh, nothing much. Just a lad who wants to see me. I'll run up in the car."

"No you won't. It may be a nut of some kind. Why don't you find out who he is?"

"Too late. Back soon."

I shuffled into my shoes, and shambled into my clothes as I stumbled downstairs. The house was cold with the chill of the half-life of 3:00 A.M. Outside the rain beat against the windows with an angry urgency. The wind whined in the fashion suitable to late January in Princeton. Drat, I said again as I thought of the sermon I had planned to.finish early in the morning. Drat to a night like this.

I tried to rush out of the back door in an attempt to escape the waterfall that raged from the gutter above the kitchen door. But the wind jammed the door against me. The primeval forces of the bleak mid-winter made sport with me, and raw-chilled rain water raced down the open collar of my coat to freeze my lately sleeping body. I puddled through a pool of winter rain and at last reached my '53 Plymouth.

The headlights barely penetrated the heavy grayness of the rain. Although the Chapel was only a few blocks from my beat-up old home, the distance seemed much longer. I turned in from Nassau Street and drove past the Firestone Library. My lights indicated the vast mass of the Chapel. I made a sweeping ninety-degree turn to the left. At the east end of the quad a white.face suddenly startled out of the blackness at the end of the lights.

"Come. Let's get out of this flood."

He said nothing but followed me meekly. I unlocked the heavy door and pulled it open against the protesting wind. Up the stairs we went to the sanctuary of my study. I turned on the lights.

"Sit down," I said as kindly as my death-at-dawn voice permitted. At last I looked at my night caller. "Quite a night, isn't it?" And sat down. "Yes?"

While I waited for his answer, I tried to understand him by observation. He sat forward in the chair, his fingers clutching the green leather of the arms. The wood paneling warmed the light. Against it his face was white. His eyes stared at me, glassy with anxiety. He wore a brown suit.

"Yes?"

"I had to see you. Just had to. Didn't know what else to do, or where to go. Things had got too much. Desperate. Desperate. Everything was crazy. I felt I'd had it. I'm scared to say it. I was going to—to kill myself. I was all set. Then I thought there might be hope, a possibility, that is. So I decided not to, and to see you. I'm in a mess—life's all broken up."

I nodded my head in sympathy. That sympathy was not unreservedly for my visitor. I had my problem. How could I help someone who was so desperate? I was just an untried harbor in a storm. What did he expect from me? What did I have to offer him?

In the pause of his monologue, he seemed to relax a little. He continued.

"There isn't any sense in what I've been saying. I'd better start at the beginning."

"That's as good a place as any. Take your time."

He moved farther back into his chair, held his hands in front of him, and started rotating rapidly a signet ring he wore on the second finger of his left hand.

"I'm a senior. I'm married, but I'm not supposed to be. You know what the situation is. If the Dean of Students knew, he'd throw me out on my neck. Everything has happened so suddenly. Early last summer I went abroad. To England. A friend took me to a big weekend party at a mansion near Winchester. What a party! It was everything I'd ever dreamed of. Cool but friendly, wild but orderly. I met this girl. We bumped into each other—literally, in the garden, in the dark. We talked. She was from New York. We even knew mutual friends. When we went inside I found she was lovely. By next morning, we were crazily in love. I mean in love. Something happened between us. Something real. It was great. Gee, it was great. After that weekend we hurried home. Saw her mother and got married."

He had settled restlessly into the chair.

"That sounds pretty good to me. Let me see, that means

you've only been married less than six months. You are still on your honeymoon!"

"Yes, we were married in August. But no, we are not on our honeymoon. That's the cause of my trouble."

"Is it?"

"Yes. I know it's hard to believe. I cannot believe it myself. But everything's gone wrong. My world's blown to pieces."

He stopped speaking and was now breathing heavily. The intensity of his anxiety increased. He rotated his ring furiously. His eyes stared at me. The muscles of his face were tight.

"So you got married? Where did you live? In Princeton?"

He did not seem to hear me, so I repeated my questions. He heard me.

"Oh, we've been living in New York."

"Aren't you supposed to live on campus?"

"Yes, sure, but I've worked out my schedule so that all my classes and precepts are in the middle of the week. I go to New York on Thursday and come back first thing on Tuesday morning. At least I did."

Silence again, silence accentuated by the rain slapping against the leaded glass. My study was like a ship's cabin in a storm. It was comfortable in the way that old-fashioned rooms sometimes are. Yet his mood did not soften. It was still hard, brittle, scared.

"Yes, I did. That's over. My Goddamn mother-in-law saw to that. The silly bitch. She fouled up her own life. Now she's fouled up ours. Would you believe it? My parents have been divorced four times. So have Maria's. God, what fools. And now her mother has done the same with us."

"How could she do that? Maria's your wife and your responsibility."

"I know. But that old bitch did not."

"What happened?"

"We didn't know how to live together. Yet hated to be apart. We got on fine in bed. But what do you do with the rest of your time? Her mother was always arranging something. We had to go to parties: cocktail parties, dinner parties, opera parties, bridge parties, weekend parties. We were pushed around, organized, displayed, patted and petted, and never allowed to be ourselves, or to be alone. For a while I didn't mind it. I thought it would end soon. It didn't. It went on and on.

"We never talked to one another except to say, 'Hello, darling,' as we passed each other at a party with a martini in our hand. We were just a couple of little wheels in a big social machine. When we went to bed in the morning we made love. But as strangers. We didn't come closer to each other. We became more distant. That made us frustrated, then angry. We were in love, but we became angry. Angry with everything. One morning Maria became so angry that she jumped out of bed, rammed on a coat, and rushed out of the house. To mother, of course. How she got to her flat I don't know. She couldn't have had any money. I thought she would come back after a sleep. But that's the hell of it. She never did. That was the end."

There was the doom of finality about that statement.

"How could that be the end?" I said, and waited until he pulled himself together again.

"How could that be the end? You don't know her mother. She's efficient, God, she's efficient. She should be the head of General Motors. Once she got Maria into her clutches, she organized her away from me. The first thing she did was to put my wife into the hands of a tamed psychiatrist. He said what the old bitch wanted him to say. She was put into one of those fancy rest homes along with a bunch of ancient cows. I don't know where the place is. Her mother gives me the run around, and the 'it's all for your good' treatment. The psychiatrist just smiles at me and offers to give me free therapy. Just knowing both of them is like being in a mad house.

"I don't know what to do. I'm imprisoned. Yesterday I tried again. I went to my lawyer. He told me to wait until Maria was cured. Cured of what? Her love for me? And that puffed-up buzzard kept telling me that she knew what was best for her daughter. Her daughter? My wife! I don't think she ever talked to her in her whole life. She's just a painted whore."

"Calm down, old boy, your mother-in-law will help you even less if you show her that this is how you feel."

"I don't think I'll ever see her again. I've had it! Almost. I came back to my room yesterday and moped around. After supper in the club I had a pint of bourbon by myself. Then I decided I'd had it, really had it. I took my gun out of my closet and loaded it. I put the muzzle against my forehead. It seemed the only sensible thing to do."

"But you didn't pull the trigger. What made you change your mind?"

"The world I've known is crazy, stupid, hellish. This is the queer part. I was reaching down to pull the trigger with my right thumb when I remembered something. Most people wouldn't think it very important. But I did."

"What did you remember?"

"I remembered having a meal with a former roommate, who graduated last year, and his wife. Suddenly I saw the whole picture so clearly. They were in love, and happy about it. Not frustrated by it as we had been. They were at ease with each other. There was something between them. Maybe it was because they weren't being pushed around by a stupid mother. Maybe it was something more. When I saw that picture I thought, maybe there is something to live for. I wanted to be with Maria. I wanted to share life with her.

"I put the gun away. I just sat there. What was I to do? I made up my mind I'd find Maria. I also decided I've got to live differently. Life isn't a party. That's all we've known, just parties. We met at a party, and we've been in a merry-go-round of parties. That's hell. Then I phoned you. I didn't know it was so late. Sorry. I know you haven't seen me before. I've never been at Chapel. But I thought you'd know what I mean, and what I'm trying to find."

"Yes, I think I do. You caught a glimpse of what it means to be human."

"I did. But how do you get that way? I thought I was human enough. Good school, good university, good connections, good old U.S. values, but they aren't good enough, are they?"

"No, they aren't."

"I knew there must be something more. That's what religion is about, isn't it? Something more. So here I am."

We continued to talk. I did most of the listening. His flow of words ended. After a period of calm, he said, "Pray for me now. Then I'll go into the Chapel to be alone, and to pray for Maria."

I prayed. He left my study and went into the darkness of the long chancel. I waited. When he returned, it was obvious that he had found peace. We left my study and walked through the rain to the University infirmary as a matter of procedure. There I introduced him to the night nurse and suggested that she give him a tranquilizer and a bed to sleep in. Later I heard he had been released after his sleep.

I picked up my car. Drove home. I opened the front door, glanced over by Palmer Stadium. A dull gray dawn was struggling to begin. It was hardly worthwhile going back to bed. I put on a kettle of water to make a pot of tea, and went into the living room to finish my sermon.

2

I SHUFFLED through the papers of my partially written sermon. The necessity of finishing it was a dull duty still to be undertaken. I reflected upon the happening of the night. A series of complex experiences had defeated a young man. According to his reckoning either he, or life, had failed, and failed so miserably, that both had lost their purpose. Because they had, there was nothing left but a deep black hole. The obvious thing was to plunge into it. Yet the obvious had not taken place. An unexpected memory of a normal, simple incident had become the messenger of hope. So powerful was this experience that a near suicide turned from death to life.

In the light of my experience I am convinced that this memory which made all the difference is an act of what we mean by the word "grace." It is another name for God's loving activity in the world. We experience this activity as something beyond our own merit, and above our own capabilities. A response is demanded of us. Our affirmative response provides meaning for existence. This response we call faith.

The undergraduate reminded me that I am a debtor of grace. I am indebted to it for my life and my freedom. There was a place, and a time, where and when I had been confronted with the finality of death. The emptiness of the conventional round of society life had introduced the undergraduate to death as a possible solution. For me it was the circumstance of war and prison camp that had brought me to the end of my physical power, and to the terminus of death.

In the death house at Chungkai on the River Kwai I had been forced to take the measure of myself as a finite human being. I had run out of life. One medical officer had said to another: "The only thing left is to let him have a decent end." That was about me! The question I had to ask myself in the death house was, "How do I get out of here?"

How did I get out? Someone came in and took me out. That man was Tom Rigden. And for no obvious reason. We had met, and like ships, sailed on. After the fall of Singapore I had escaped in a ship I had taken over from the Royal Navy. My destination was Sumatra. On the way I picked up a naval officer who had been shipwrecked by enemy action. In Sumatra we joined forces and organized an escape service. We continued in partnership until the fall of Sumatra was imminent. He stayed behind as the naval liaison officer at Padang, in the forlorn hope that a ship of the Royal Navy might make a heroic effort to rescue survivors; while I went on in a sailing boat to Ceylon. I never made it. The Japanese Navy got in the way. We met again in the death house. And then only because this naval officer, Tom Rigden, sought me out, and found me.

Why he should have done so is a mystery. We had known each other briefly. We had little in common. I was a Scot, he an Englishman. I was in the infantry, he in the navy. There were fellow officers who could have been concerned about me, but who were not. Tom Rigden was.

He found me paralyzed and knocking at the door of death. Having done so, he arranged for me to be carried out of the death house. I was taken to a clean little lean-to. There I was nursed by Dusty Miller and Dinty Moore. These were men he had asked to help me. I knew that he had done this. It was not until the fall of 1965, twenty-three years after the event, that I learned he had done much more.

After a summer vacation I arrived back in Princeton. On my desk was a letter from Kuala Lumpur, in Malaysia. The sender was E. M. Stewart. We were friends in Malaya. We were also fellow prisoners at Chungkai. Immediately after the war Helen and I shared a large flat with him and his bride in Edinburgh.

I was delighted to see by the postmark and address who the letter was from. I opened it and read:

My dear Ernest,

A lot of water has run under a lot of bridges since 1945/46!—and a lot of friends who were with us then are no longer here! But it was pleasant to see your name on "Miracle on the River Kwai"—was it, perhaps? only last year! Anyway, I bought—well brought up, me—a copy and read it with great interest, as you'll imagine. It's not often that one finds oneself mentioned in a book so it was a second pleasant surprise. I had intended to write to you then and congratulate you on the book, etc., but that never got done—like so many things in life! "Anything you can put off until tomorrow, put off for good!" Anyway I sent the book home to my son.

One of the things that made me believe that your memories of Siam, circa 1944, are fading was brought back to me a few weeks ago when an Australian salesman called on me. It emerged that he had been in the timber business in Sarawak and when he asked if I'd ever come across a P.O.W. in Siam named Tom Rigden, it wouldn't have required the proverbial feather. Rigden had worked for this man in Sarawak.

That was an omission in your book which made me feel that you'd forgotten some things—like us all. Do you remember when you were lying in the little outhouse under the eaves of one of the Chungkai huts, very, very ill with amoebic and malaria and lots more, and you needed emetine? Well, Rigden sold his gold Rolex (through me) to a Jap for—I think—120 ticals, which was enough to get for you the extra emetine over and above what Ian Mackintosh subscribed. That saved your life, Ernest! You were so ill that you couldn't remember—but it was a great example of—next door to—"giving up one's life" on Rigden's part.

I was moved. I could hardly believe what I had read. Tom Rigden had done all this for me? In those days a gold Rolex watch was better than a field of Texas oil wells. Thai merchants valued it as the prince of watches and paid accordingly. None was available for purchase except the rare one or two that belonged to lucky prisoners.

Tom Rigden sold his watch of great price in order to buy emetine for me. That was something!

Emetine is a medicine essential to the cure of amoebic dysentery. This disease had cursed me for two years. It drained me of blood and of the meager nourishment I received from our tiny ration of rice.

I was dying. The first step away from the grave was the cure of this bloody flux.

I remember my friend, Ian Mackintosh of the Royal Army Medical Corps, visiting me in my miserable little shack. "Ernest," he said, "we think you might make it. But only if we can cure this bloody dysentery. I think we can."

"How?"

"With emetine! We've been able to buy some through the black market. Enough to give you twelve shots. That's the minimum we may use effectively. I could use at least a thousand times that amount. There are so many who need it."

"But why me?" I looked at him in surprise. "If there are so many, give it to someone else. I'll be all right. With a bit of luck, I'll make it."

"Like hell you will. You've had all the luck you'll ever have.

It's emetine, chum, that you need now. Your days of being tough are over. You may still end up as a corpse. Without emetine it is certain that you will within the next two weeks. I know there are some worse than you. It's too late for them. Anyway, this lot of emetine is for you. And do you know what?"

"No! What?"

"Some of us think that you can do something worth while with your life after this is all over. That's why we are prepared to take a gamble that you'll live."

I looked around my little shack. It was about seven feet long, six feet high where it was fastened to the wall of the main hut, and about four feet broad. Through its tiny door I could see the beaten-down earth of the compound and the dreary brown attap of the next hut. There was nothing within sight to suggest a future, far less one that was worth while. Such a future was too much at odds with my present to take it seriously. I felt like laughing at the absurdity of his optimism. The face bending over mine, however, was serious, kindly, concerned, sympathetic. I did not laugh. Instead I said rather quietly, "You do?"

"Yes, I do!"

"And the emetine? How can you get that through the black market just for me?"

"That's my problem, not yours. What you have to do is to get well. And don't forget it."

I said nothing. I just looked at him. "My God," I thought. "What a decent guy."

That emetine came as an undeserved gift. I could not guess who was responsible for it. I had not the faintest idea that it was Tom Rigden. Ian Stewart was right. It was "next door to —giving up one's life": for Tom, among other things, had asthma, tuberculosis, and amoebic dysentery. Never once did he hint that he had made the medicine possible.

This reminder of that "greater love" recalled the trust that Ian Mackintosh had expressed in me: "*You can do something* worth while with your life." That embarrassed me. Me! Do something worth while? He little realized what was in my mind. What did he mean by worth while?

My plans for the future could be called worth while only by highly ambitious and aggressive types, but not by such sensitive men as Ian and Tom. "Worth while" was not in my scheme of things. I fancied a touch of power: a position of influence within some power structure. It could hardly be England: for that was all in the hands of the Harrow or Eton boys. I saw a future for a lad of parts in the East. A touch of power doesn't have to be white. The changing patterns of the Orient had already cast their shadows and I had seen some of them.

After Ian had left, I was haunted by his phrase. I was angry with him, for being so sentimental. Worth while be damned! But the question remained, what? What the devil was worth while? I had lost the few possessions I had acquired by wit. And all I had to go back to was about $350 in the bank. Just enough for a decent weekend on the town. Ian's interpretation of worth while did not suggest the possibility of enlarging my credit.

That worth while bit kept troubling me like an annoying toothache. Whatever it might mean in the future, it seemed to me that prison camp was a poor preparation. We had nothing but hard work, starvation, disease, brutality, and the struggle for life, a struggle that could be questioned. What was there to live for?

The emetine had worked. My paralyzed body began to stir again. The pain of the ulcers on my legs was the first sign of the returning life. But the question, "What shall I do that is worth while?" was even more painful than my sores.

A burst of sunlight filled my study. A little stained-glass cross on a window shone like a jewel of rubies and sapphires. The student visiting me was saying, "I've been here for nearly four years. I'm going on to law school. I've learned lots of things except how to do something worth while with my life.

That's my problem, Dean Gordon, where is life to be learned?"

"Where? Wherever you are, son. You begin by accepting life as a gift. The whole of it. There are times when you may not like it. But when you feel that way, you still cannot return the ticket to existence. By accepting life, your life: suffering and joy, fear and love, anxiety and faith, time and eternity, man and God, you will understand something of the glory of life's mystery. Dig your feet down into the dust. Get muddy and wet and hurt. But don't look at the dust and the mud all the time. Look up, and look around. Look at the beauty that is everywhere. Look at the goodness there is in people. Look at the stars. Look and be silent. In the silences of moments of wonder you will hear the word that only God may speak. Do you know what word I mean?"

"I'm not sure that I do. Do you mean that it is something that this university can't initiate? Something that is beyond anything we can say for ourselves?"

"Yes. And you know the word. Love."

My first appreciation of the prison camp was wrong. It was a place where I learned about life. I learned a little law, a little philosophy, and a little about literature as well. But for me it was essentially the university of life.

I learned to accept life, conscious as I did so that it was a costly gift. I was a victim of grace. The question, *What to do?* still remained.

One day an Australian sergeant, a former middle-weight boxer, visited me in my shack. He wanted me to lead a discussion group on the Christian faith. The object was simple. It was to find out if Christianity was true or not. Maybe it offered a better way than we realized. The acceptable way of the world was lousy. It was dog-eat-dog and kick a man in the teeth when he is down. Disarmed by his charming honesty, I told him I'd give it a go.

The men with whom I met surprised me. They were honest, keen, kindly, brave. They were responding in their way to a challenge and a hope. They were reaching beyond their environment. I was the teacher. Yet I was the one who did the learning. I was hauled out of my clean, icy tower of thought. The security of my objectivity was destroyed. I was exposed to life with all my nerve ends showing.

By their trust those men introduced me to the dimension of faith in which I needed much schooling. They honored me by taking me into their lives. What was so disturbingly humiliating was that they loved me. All the time I was becoming the victim of grace.

I saw myself clearly in an incident that occurred at Nakawm Paton. This was the camp for the very sick to which I had been sent after Chungkai. In the same hut there was an English officer who prided himself on his cynicism. Reason was ultimate; faith absurd. I saw him being carried into the hut in a makeshift stretcher. He was filthy. His beard straggled weakly from his scrawny face. His legs were a mess of festering ulcers. And his manner was as offensive as his stench.

Two volunteer orderlies took care of him. They were members of the community of faith. They fed him, cleaned him, nursed him. As they did so he mocked them. They listened, smiled, and continued to care for him.

We were brothers that man and I: victims of grace. We believed in reason and rational processes. But these were not saving us. The love of faithful men was.

The men of faith entangled me in the net of grace. Because they did, they directed me toward one answer to the question, "What ought I to do that is worth while?" That answer was: a proclaimer of the Gospel. It was not an easy answer for me. I viewed the prospects with dismay. I had enjoyed military service. I liked adventure. I was at ease in the company of tough and aggressive men. I was very reluctant to exchange the kilt for the cassock, and the sword for the pen.

As soon as I returned from the jungle I took up the study of theology at Edinburgh. My first impressions almost caused me to return immediately to the jungle. On a visit to St. Andrews I went to church in the evening. I was in uniform. Five minutes before the service began I looked into the building—a lovely one. About fifteen people were sitting self-consciously apart from each other. Jokingly, I asked the elder at the door, "I suppose I can help myself to a seat?" The elder looked at me and replied, "Take whichever seat you fancy, Captain." I sat down. A minute later two elderly ladies tapped me on the shoulder to say, "Excuse me, sir, you are sitting in our seat." I moved two rows forward.

Not only was Edinburgh too cold for my thin blood, but many of the churchly people were too coldly proper and respectable for my passionate view of life. On top of it all, my allowance only paid half of the rent. And my hero's gratuity of a hundred quid or so was shrinking. The jungle was so appealing. Two very good prospects turned up which would have enabled me to return.

"I've chosen the wrong answer, Lord," I said. "I can't see anything worth while in those hopelessly involved theological constructions, nor in those black-suited servants of righteousness smelling of mothballs and peppermint. How about letting me have a go at something else?"

I had to give up our flat for lack of money. I started packing my tropical kit.

A chance acquaintance heard of my plight and suggested that I call up a minister friend of his. I did. Helen and I were invited to tea.

The manse was a large house of red sandstone. It faced Arthur's Seat, the hillock in Edinburgh which marks the climax of the King's Park. The tea was excellent, our host jovial. Several times I asked him if he knew of an apartment at a reasonable rent. He brushed aside my question with the remark, "We can talk of that later." Later appeared to be getting later and later. At last, we indicated that we would have to be on our way. If we did not find a flat by evening, we would leave Edinburgh.

"What's your hurry," remarked our host. "Don't you like our place?"

"Of course we do. But what do you mean?"

"We assumed you would stay here. You can have the second floor. It is big enough."

"Great!" we exclaimed. "What is the rent?"

"Would ten shillings be too much? That will include gas and electricity, of course."

Our last rent had been five pounds a week. I had to haggle the price up to a pound.

Our new landlord was Gordon Livingston. Because of him, I said, "All right, Lord, I'll give this another go." While I was learning theology, Greek, Hebrew, etc., at theological college, I was learning more about the Christian faith from him.

One evening I went into his sitting room for a chat. A tramp was sitting on a chair with the leg of his trousers rolled up. Gordon was kneeling beside him bathing a varicose ulcer. When the ugly wound was dressed, he bound it with an elastoplast bandage. He looked up with a hearty smile. "Someone gave me this bandage. I kept it because there is always a use for every gift."

After a supper of boiled mutton and potatoes, the man went off with two pounds from Gordon in his pocket.

"Why did you give him that?" I asked. "Isn't he taking you for a sucker?"

"Oh no! These tramps have a hard time of it. Edinburgh is a hard city. That is why he wanted to move on to Newcastle. With that ulcer he shouldn't walk. I gave him money for the train. Mebbe he'll find a job when he gets there. Mebbe he'll stay with a friend. Who knows what he'll do. He doesn't. Tramps are like Christians. They live a day at a time. They have no abiding city; and keep looking for the one that is to come."

On a freezing day in the hard winter of 1947, I returned from my classes eager for a cup of tea. Gordon was waiting in the hall.

"Could you spare a wee bit coal?"

"Certainly."

We went to the cellar. It was woefully empty. There was a

little heap on our side, and less on his. He had brought a wooden apple box with him. We filled it. Gordon nailed it down and wrote a name and address on the lid. "Now give me a hand with this." We carried it to the nearest tram car halt and waited until one grated to a stop. We loaded it onto the driver's platform. Gordon paid the appropriate fare and off it rattled.

"What was that all about?"

"Oh, didn't I tell you? The milkman told me this morning that old Mr. Macdonald had run out of his ration. His wife, poor soul, has had pneumonia. That wasn't much we gave him, but it will help."

"Do you know Mr. Macdonald?"

"No, no, but the milkman does."

Gordon was loved by old folk, children, and tramps. He was also loved by the Communists at the Mound. The Mound is just off Princes Street. On Saturday nights it is an open forum for the champions of causes.

One Saturday Gordon stood in the crowd, listening to a Communist present an eloquent appeal for social justice in the world. He challenged the crowd to a debate. He stepped down from his podium and offered it to any possible contender. Gordon pushed his way through and stood on the platform. He was an elderly clergyman in cast-off clothes. Yet he was an impressive sight. His face was strong and his words sincere.

He began:

"I agree with my friend. Justice is not the execution of law for the sake of the privileged few. It is loving people. The best justice this world has ever seen was lived out by a working man in Palestine. He brought his justice to those who were the victims of injustice. The church, the government, and the army executed him. But they could not kill his justice. That goes on. No one can stop it. It is good men like you who can bring justice to others. I can see that you are concerned about those who haven't had a square deal.

"God is concerned, too. Mebbe that is why you are concerned. When we love we are sharing his love. That is the power which makes justice work.

"As you can hear, I'm not disagreeing with my friend. I'm for him. But don't forget justice means loving people."

His face glowed with his compassion. His spectacles reflected the street lights in miniature. He stood tall with dignity. He was not simply an elderly minister dressed in old, badly fitting clothes. He was an inspired disciple of that Jewish workman. He paused. A pause which held his audience in the silence of attention. Then he concluded:

"I did not begin with a text, but I'll end with one. 'For God sent the Son into the world, not to condemn the world, but to set it free.' We've just come through the condemnation of war. That is something we did, because of our fear and our hate. God does not condemn. He loves."

He stopped. When he stepped down he seemed to shrink a little. The leader of the group stood up.

"That'll be all for tonight. I want the Reverend to know that he'll be welcome to speak here at any time."

I learned much about God's grace from Gordon. He was a beautiful man. Before studying for the ministry he had been a cavalry officer.

My time at Edinburgh and my G.I. allowance came to an end. I had nowhere to go. I had applied for a chaplaincy in the R.A.F. My application had been favorably received. I was assured of an appointment. Shortly before graduation, I received a curt note telling me that the number of vacancies for that year had been cut. There was no place for me.

I became the skipper of a large sailing yacht. The salary helped to pay my bills, and the quietness of night sailing underlined my question, "What do I do that is worth while?"

After a trip the yacht was lying alongside the jetty. Helen came down waving a piece of paper in her hand. "There's a letter from America for you. I thought you'd better read it right away."

I read it. Tertius van Dyke, Dean of the Hartford Theological Seminary, informed me that I had been awarded a fellow-ship.

"What do you think of this?" I asked as I handed the letter to Helen.

She smiled. "Great! When do we take off?"

"Didn't say anything about you, did it?"

"Didn't need to. I'm coming."

Passages were in short supply. I worked my passage to Sydney, Nova Scotia, raced at Oyster Bay in a British six-meter for the Scandinavian Gold Cup, and matriculated at Hartford. Helen followed in a troop ship.

Two and a half years later we returned to Scotland. Now we were three. We had a six-week-old daughter, Gillian. I was ordained in Paisley Abbey where I served as an assistant minister. After two years I reckoned it was time to move on. But where? I had applied for a position in a Japanese university that was in the process of being organized. Its opening, how-ever, was postponed for several years, and my plans thwarted.

I was concerned about the institutional church. It was living in a fool's paradise. It was not living in the twentieth century. Bishops, in their councils, were talking about theological and historical absurdities, while statesmen were preparing for an-other clean little war. Presbyteries were concerned about pre-serving ancient monuments, while youngsters were left leader-less in the slums. Churchmen were talking, while the world was dying. Those who were *in* the church were angry with those who were *out* because they did not come *in*. The angrier they became the more they kept the *out* out. That seemed daft to me.

There were not enough men *in* so I tried to go out to where they were. I could not blame them for staying out. The at-mosphere was not masculine enough. Lonely for a bit of honest company, I started dropping into some of the pubs in the par-ish for a glass of ale. Before my glass was half empty, I had a crowd round my table. I was asked honest questions. Some of the questioners dropped into church once in a while.

Another thing I did was to serve as a combatant officer in the local Territorial Battalion of the Argyll and Sutherland Highlanders. Men felt free to talk to me because I was one of them. I also met a few of my old comrades. They had taken up weekend soldiering as a hobby.

I was interested to note the difference that existed between the young and the old soldiers. It was the difference of experience. At a military exercise, I overheard an unbloodied hero say to an old friend who had been wounded in the same battle as myself:

"You old soldiers don't know what war is all about. You know nothing about strategy. All you ever did was to fix bayonets and make a mad rush in the direction of the enemy. By the time you got there they weren't there."

"So you know all about that, do you? How do you know?"

"I use my head. I read books."

"And that means you know about war, does it?"

"Sure it does."

My friend unbuttoned his khaki wool shirt and pulled it over his head.

"Now, show me your wounds!"

The right arm, shoulder, and back were pitted with wound scars. The incident reminded me of a remark made by St. Paul, "Don't let anybody bother me. I bear the scars of my service to Jesus on my body." It also reminded me of a line from one of Archibald MacLeish's poems, which is dear to me, "Men are brothers by life lived and are hurt for it."

It was at an army camp at the end of summer that I realized what the next move was to be. Before I left the United States an executive of the Presbyterian Church suggested that I should stay in the country. My reply was in the negative. He asked me if I would not be willing to consider some form of work. On the spur of the moment I said, "Oh, I might consider some type of college work."

I had received a letter from this executive. It was a gracious one. He expressed the belief that I would soon find a college position if I returned to the States as soon as possible.

One early morning as I lay on my camp bed, I again considered the question, "What shall I do?"

It was an unusually bright and clear morning for an English summer. The flaps of the tent were open. The scents of the earth perfumed the cool breeze. My view from the tent was open and fresh: lush green grass, a clump of pine trees, and a clean blue sky. I kicked over my rough army blankets, felt the friendly texture of the grass with my feet, and said, "Why not!" Whatever was for life, and youth, and hope was good.

The duty piper called the rest of the camp from its sleep with *Hey, Johnny Cope, are ye waken yet.* Before he had finished, my letter was written to the executive, saying that he could expect me to arrive within the next three months.

With regret, I informed Bill Rogan of my decision. He was the minister of the twelfth-century kirk. Our association had been a happy one. From him I learned that there are great opportunities in the parish ministry, particularly when the church is compassionately concerned for those within its parish.

During the last month of my ministry a man approached me after the evening service.

"Do you mind if I have a word with you?"

"Of course not. Come into my room for a chat."

He was a healthy-looking young man: short, but strong. His face was keen and intelligent.

"I've been giving the beadle a hand with the doors at night." This meant that he opened the heavy doors to let latecomers in, and closed them again to keep out the noise of the High Street. He looked at me directly.

"I've been doing this for the last month; just to give Sam a break. He's a friend. It is the first time I've been in church in the last ten years. I like what you have to say. I've been doing a lot of thinking about it. You see, I'm secretary of my union. The Communist Party want me to join them. They've promised me an executive position if I do. I was ready to join. Then I heard you. What I've been looking for in Communism isn't there. It's in the Christian faith. I know that now, and I'm grateful to you for helping me see it. I'll not be pushed around by an ideology. I'll be concerned for the people I represent. That way I'll be able to help them better."

He stood up, dour and determined in his navy blue trench coat.

"I hear you're leaving. You'll be missed. Best of luck to you." With that he walked out of the Abbey into the streets of Paisley.

At the end of November, 1952, we sailed for New York. There were four of us. Alastair was nine months old. The restrictions of the sterling exchange limited our financial assets drastically. There was no position waiting for me. Only Gillian was uncertain. She did not want to leave her Granny.

A friendly customs officer in New York took pity on our young family and heavy luggage. He pushed us through with the minimum of trouble and the maximum of kindness. My name was called out and a letter presented to me. It informed me that I was expected at the Presbyterian Church of Amagansett for a month as a supply minister. After a lot of inquiry, I discovered that this village was at the far end of Long Island on the south shore.

When we went out there by train, it seemed to be at the end of the world. As we journeyed on, the crowded train emptied. The last passenger left at Southampton and we were on our own. Apprehensively, we watched the landscape of sand dune and black pine pass us by. There was less and less of anything. Alastair started the journey in a white fur coat. By the time the trainman shouted, "Amagansett next," it was as black as the carriage floor on which he had been crawling.

Amagansett seemed next to nowhere. It was beautiful, however, and it has become even more beautiful through the years. But the nearest university was so far away that I was unlikely to hear of it, far less it hear of me. We had left one of the biggest church buildings in Scotland and arrived at one of the smallest in the States. Helen reminded me of this, and suggested that perhaps it would cure me of my wild enthusiasms. We had agreed that if a college appointment did not materialize, we would return within a few years. This seemed reasonable enough. I loved sand and sea, but that was not what seemed to be worth while in the prison camp connotation.

Our first month passed. The church session asked me to accept a call. When I declined and told them why, they were very understanding. They were willing to put up with me until I was called to college work.

Our first evening in the manse was not inspiring. There were few lamps. These were lit by 40-watt bulbs. The rooms had probably been used for church school, and someone had forgotten to sweep up afterward.

We had just put our babies to bed when there was a knock on the door. Our visitor was a wiry old man. His face was lean and weatherbeaten. His glasses rested at the bottom of a long nose. I welcomed him in.

"I don't want to interrupt anything. You'll be wanting to get your unpacking done. I'm your neighbor. I do a little bit of farming. I've brought over a few eggs, a quart of milk, a drop of cream, and I've some kindling outside. A nice fire will brighten things up."

Without the fire the house was brighter.

One of my first telephone calls was from a woman who wanted to know if I would allow her to attend the services.

"Of course, you are most welcome," I said when I visited her immediately after the call.

"You'd better not say that until you hear my story."

"That won't make any difference, whatever it is. You'll still be welcome."

"When I came here I lived with a man. He was married. He kept telling me that his divorce would be coming through soon. When it did, we'd be married right away. Time kept passing. He kept saying the same thing. I discovered he was going with another woman at the same time he was living with me. Then he left me. I was alone. I was frightened to be seen in the village. Everyone must have known what had been going on. I stayed in the house and fretted. I couldn't stand my loneliness any longer. I took poison. A neighbor brought in the paper. Found me on the floor. Called the police. I was rushed to Southampton Hospital.

"When I came back the house was empty. Empty! It was my furniture. He took everything. I wonder if you know what it is like to come to nothing? Just nothing."

She sat in a straight-back chair. She looked ill, blanched white with fear and loneliness. Her hands plucked at the rug she was mending.

"I decided to finish it. To do a good job this time."

"But you didn't. What happened?"

"I think God must have had mercy on me. Do you know Emil Gardell?"

"Of course I do. He's my neighbor and Alastair's best friend."

"He came to visit me. There I was, standing in the middle of this empty room."

"I bet I know what he said. 'Here's a few eggs and a drop of cream.' "

She smiled.

"He did. He looked around and said, 'Well, I do declare. You could do with a few things around here. I've some things in my barn that I've no use for. You'll do me a favor if you take them in. I'll harness up Molly and Polly and bring them round.' "

I looked around. "Are these his few things?"

"Yes. They are."

"You've taken good care of them. But tell me, why do you feel that you are not welcome in church?"

"Because of what I am. I'm no good."

"That's what the church is for."

"What do you mean?"

"It's for those who think that they are no good. People who think they are good don't need God's help."

"I'm glad you think it's all right: for I need his help so much."

A year passed. In the spring of 1954, I received a letter from the chairman of the Trustees of the Westminster Foundation at Princeton. My name had been given to him by a fellow minister of the Long Island Presbytery. Would I be interested in the position of the directorship? It meant taking pastoral care of Presbyterian students. Helen and I talked it over. We decided to give it a try.

Shortly after Hurricane Carol, we left for Princeton. I was going to miss the fishing.

I was surprised to find how gracious the university administration was to denominational chaplains. I liked the campus. After a time, however, I knew that I would not care to carry on with that kind of work for very long. The answer seemed to lie in a new appointment that had been offered me. It was that of serving a large church situated on the edge of a campus.

While I was making up my mind to accept, I received a telephone call from President Harold Dodds of Princeton.

"Are you free about four this afternoon? If you are I'd like you to come and have a cup of tea with me."

I replied that I was, and that I would.

I had tea with the President in his study at Prospect. After we had exchanged pleasantries and finished our tea, he said,

"As you know, Donald Aldrich resigned as Dean of the Chapel last January. I wonder if you would like to think about accepting the deanship. I'll give you a call in a week or so."

I left Prospect with the promise that I would think about this offer so graciously presented to me.

I had come to the United States to work with students. I had anticipated being sent to one of the Presbyterian colleges. I thought that the Westminster Foundation was a step on the way. In Princeton's past there was a humble and religious origin. The College of New Jersey was founded in 1746 as a child of the *Great Awakening*. This was a truly evangelical movement that took grace seriously. I found warmth in this knowledge. I was not so sure about its twentieth-century air of sophistication. Like the other colleges, damned with prestige, it was given a haze of suburban affluence. This has sometimes been mistaken for reality.

The great Neo-Gothic Chapel was both a menace and a blessing. Its size was overpowering. How could it be filled with sound and people? Yet, it challenged the campus.

The students with whom I worked were intelligent and concerned. They were the opposite of the Princeton stereotype of fiction. They were capable human beings.

The campus offered a great challenge. Better than I had envisioned. Bigger than I could cope with.

At the end of the week, President Dodds called me again. I told him how delighted I was to have this privilege of carrying on my ministry at Princeton University. I could foresee that I would have a great deal of uncertainty to contend with. But this was something to which I was accustomed.

3

IT WAS one thing to believe that the campus was God's place for me; it was another to minister in it effectively. I calculated the disadvantages. They were many.

It was 1955. The Back to God Movement was at its height. This movement worried me. When I was brought to the bondage of Changi Prison Camp in Singapore, there was a Back to God revival in progress. I was critical of it in those days because of my antireligious sentiments. In 1955, I was critical of the movement because what it stood for was not true to my experiences, nor to the insights provided by the Christian faith.

The movement repeated the mistake made by the Old Testament prophets: that of claiming that all modern men had to do was to turn to God and all would be well. The nation would be blessed with peace and plenty. Life is too complex for such simple optimism. Some of the best men I have ever known were not rewarded for their faith, but killed. Is not that what happened to Jesus?

In the uncertain aftermath of World War II, Korea and the United States' new global involvement, I could see why citizens felt the need to turn to someone. Just as in the prison camps of my time men, deprived of their old props, turned to God, so did the nation. This tells us something about men and nations. But not about God. He is not in their pay, and he cannot be confined to a back room of the White House.

I estimated that this movement would create problems for two reasons.

One: it said the wrong thing about God. He was misinterpreted as the big Sugar Daddy, Big Brother, the boss guy who punishes you when you are naughty, and gives you a lollipop when you are good. Because it said the wrong thing about God, it helped to originate the wrong arguments about him. Because they were wrong they discredited him.

Two: it stressed a reactionary view of history. We do not go back to God. He is not behind us in the mists of Sinai nor the suburbs of the old Puritan Boston. He is always ahead of us. We go forward to him.

These two factors had an inhibiting influence on the life of faith. No sooner had I started preaching in the Chapel than I received angry letters from pious alumni accusing me of impiety. They were in a minority, it is true, yet they represented the old diehards who stick to an authoritarian God of law, or else to a chairman of the board type, who rewards the successful. It is easy to see why their views have created the credibility and generation gaps. Undergraduates were bound to turn against their distorted picture of God. Some did. They rejected the picture because they saw it to be insincere.

I found myself often involved in lengthy discussions with undergraduates who believed they were atheists.

"How can you believe such junk?" one undergraduate asked me in my study.

"What junk?"

"All this junk about God. I've come to talk to you about why *I* don't believe in him. Faith is one of the biggest exercises in self-deception and intellectual dishonesty. There are no conclusive proofs for God. Maybe there aren't any against him, but there aren't any for him. That is a certainty. Because you can't prove God's existence you are left with faith. That's worse than nothing. You may say that you believe in God, but when I ask you, 'What sort of God?' you can't tell me."

"Can't I?"

"No, you can't."

"Suppose I say I can?"

"I don't believe you can."

"Maybe so. I can at least be true to the insights faith has given me. I've learned that God is love. This is the word Jesus brought to the world. He lived that word. He taught us how to do the same. Whatever God is like, he is like Jesus."

"That proves nothing."

"I did not say it did. I merely was beginning to answer your question, 'What sort of God?' "

"That doesn't mean much. You can believe in anything that way: in Jesus Christ, in the Buddha, in Allah, in V. I. Lenin, in Hitler. In other words, God is a product of our minds. Voltaire said that 'if God made us in his image, we have certainly returned the compliment.' I believe that."

"I agree with you that many of us try to create God in our own likeness. I daresay we're all guilty of doing so. But God is always bigger than our ideas of him."

"No, he isn't. Our ideas grow out of our education, conditioning, and experience. Men have always had a president, or a king, or a tribal chief. Because they have, they get this idea that there has to be a number one, the big chief over everything. I hear people say that God is omnipotent and benevolent. They say that because they form the idea that someone must be the boss. At the same time they want someone who'll be kind to them, tough with everyone else, but kind with them. That's crazy. If God were omnipotent and benevolent, he could not allow all the terrible suffering there is in the world."

"I'm not in a position to say what he can or cannot do. I cannot know the mind of God, neither can I tell him what he ought or ought not to do. What I can do is to respond to him

in the mystery by which he reveals himself, and in the challenge of Jesus as his word of love."

"These are just words. What religious people want is something to go back on. It is back to the womb, or back to some
imagined security in the past."

"Some people may want that. I don't. One of the reasons
why we can't prove God is because we can't pin him down on
a dissecting board, nor confine him to a corner in the past. He
is, and he is ever becoming. He is not in the security of our
laws, but in the uncertainty of our faith. But I'm not sure
there is too much point in talking about him. The point is
in following him. He is the author of life. The only proof I
know is in the quality of our lives. Maybe we know him in
the life lived. No one has the last word on him. Not even
you."

I said that because I've never known anyone who has won
an argument on the subject "God," but I have known men
who have been won by the quality of other men's lives. "Back
to God" was too weak a formula for the complexities of contemporary life. The word "God" in general referred to the
status quo as people believed it to be. This heresy could only
encourage young men to ask the wrong questions, and religious
people to give the wrong answers.

This backward look, the same kind as that of Lot's wife, had
its political manifestations. Senator Joseph McCarthy had just
been prevented from taking over from God. His shadow, however, still darkened the land. Anti-Communism was the big
slogan around which the forces of self-righteousness were rally-
ing. It was dangerous to be for freedom, truth, love, and man.
It was dangerous to be for God unless it was the God of laissez-
faire capitalism, America firsters, me firsters, and the believers'
dark gnawing dread of the future.

Honest dialogue was stifled on the campus. There was a
fear of saying the first word. The mood was conservative: conservation of the values of impersonalism, and the exaltation of
law over man. Undergraduates were expected to be seen and

not heard, and to follow along the success-blazed trail of their elders. No wonder they were called *The Silent Generation.* The establishment had determined that for them. After a campus storm in a tea cup, one alumnus wrote to tell me that I was failing in my job. My job was to make undergraduates good. This is the big-stick approach of the Nazis, "beat the slobs until they know what is good for them." I had not read of this approach in the New Testament.

The backward look was also based upon an anxiety about the future. That anxiety resulted in the conservation of values, which should have been buried a long time ago. I believe that it was because of this attitude of fear that the Civil Rights movement was held back.

I had come to the United States about the time of the bus strike in Montgomery, Alabama. From what I read in the newspapers, I learned to admire Martin Luther King. For me he was one of the rare prophetic voices in the land. We corresponded for a time. He agreed to preach for me in the fall of 1959. That was when he was stabbed in New York. He came a year later. He was one of the most loving and gracious men I have known.

When I met him at the Trenton Station, an undergraduate who was with me asked him, "Why don't you have a bodyguard? After your attack of last year I didn't think you would go anywhere without one." Martin Luther King's face shone with a smile.

"I don't need a bodyguard. I'm in the Lord's hands. My time is his time. He knows what I have to do, and when." His sermon that morning was on the power of love. This, he stressed, was the only power that would enable men to cross over the racial boundaries. As it was true of the white man, it was also true of the black man. Both had to face each other and see themselves in God's eyes.

The impressions I gained from Martin Luther King were confirmed when I met with his father on the Monday before his son's funeral. He spoke lovingly of him. "M. L. was always such a gracious boy. The devil would get into me and I'd give him a row. I'd even spank him. M. L. would just never say a word. He stood there with the tears rolling down his face. He loved me. He never stopped loving me. He never stopped loving anybody. Why, I remember when he was but a little boy, and we lived in the country, he met some families that had been thrown out of their shacks. M. L. came to see me at a meeting of my deacons. He told us about them so well that all my deacons were weeping. So, because of young M. L., the church took care of these families. We took them all into our houses. That's what M. L. was always doing, taking people in."

As I listened to Martin Luther King, Sr., I understood why. Here was a Christian man, one who lived the Gospel. He was strong in his faith. He went on: "Forgive me for talking so much. I've got to keep talking. If I don't I'll cry. I guess M. L. always knew what would happen. He'd be late for a meeting because he'd met someone. He was always late. I'd give him a telling off. He'd just smile. I know why he was always late. He had so much to do, and so little time. He had only thirty-eight years."

As I stood listening to the father in that living room of the Kings, I saw the beauty of the Gospel; that beauty which the black people have seen so much more clearly than we white folks. I saw young M. L. as a disciple of the man of love with so much to do and so little time. I remembered how he had requested as the sermon hymn:

> Once to every man and nation
> Comes the moment to decide. . . .
> Standeth God within the shadow
> Keeping watch above his own.

The response of the undergraduates who heard Martin Luther King was all that I expected it to be. They heard what he was, and were touched by him. The serenity of his spirit spoke to them.

"I'm from the South," said an undergraduate to me after

the service. "I've always been proud of our history. I'm not any more. It hurts to think of it. My God, what have we done? How many Martin Luther Kings have we insulted, rejected, and ignored? What stupidity! We need them more than they need us."

This enlightened attitude was not shared by our alumni. A few thought that a committee ought to be formed to supervise the choice of Chapel preachers. One Southern gentleman came up to my wife at a meeting on campus to say, "We don't like what your husband is doing to the Chapel."

"What do you mean?" My wife, as a Scot, has all the strength of a nation that has taken freedom seriously for over a thousand years. She would not be intimidated by angry tigers who hid behind insincere smiles.

"I mean what everybody knows. Your husband deliberately invited a political agitator to speak from the pulpit of the Chapel. Do you know of any reason why he should be allowed to remain?"

"I do. For the very good reason that there are people who still think as you do. You ought to listen to him sometime."

This demonic attitude had a frightening influence on some undergraduates. One came to see me.

"I'm here to say good-by. I've got to leave."

I was perplexed; he was a good man and a good student.

"That's the wrong thing to say. You're only a sophomore. You can't be in academic or disciplinary trouble. What's biting you?"

"My dad has cut me off."

"Cut you off? That's the daftest thing I've ever heard. He can't do that."

"He has."

"Why?"

"Last Thanksgiving I went home. I took my roommate with me. He's Chinese. When I was getting ready to return to campus, my dad asked me to see him in his study. He told me that I had been learning some no-good things at Princeton.

The first of these was rooming with a Chinese. He said he respected the Chinese and knew that they had enough pride to keep to themselves. Chinese are good as Chinese, and whites are good as whites, but we have to respect each other. We do that by keeping to ourselves."

"How did you answer that?"

"I told him I respected people. That meant liking them. When you like them you know them as people, and not as Chinese, or rich, or poor."

"What was your dad's answer to that?"

"He got angry. Real angry. He told me I was all wrong. There's different kinds of people. There's our kind, and their kind. He asked me what I thought of Nigras."

"And you told him?"

"That they were people just like him or anyone else."

"He didn't like that, did he?"

"That was the big blowup. He said that Princeton was obviously so rotten that it let people like me associate with 'them.' He described 'them' as worse than dogs. 'I'll let my dogs come into the house, but damn you'll never see one of those field Nigras, not even in my kitchen.'

"I didn't leave on good terms. Dad and Mom keep writing to me, pleading with me to change my mind and come back home with my own people. Here, this is the kind of letter I've been getting from my mother."

He handed me a letter. I read it. It was the cruelest blackmail I've ever come across.

> You don't know how much you are breaking your Daddy's heart and mine by thinking and writing as you do. We are good people. We've been in ——— for a long time. Your granddaddy gave the town a college. We've been in politics. Daddy pays the minister's salary. How can you do this to us? We've given you everything. We've made sacrifices for your good. I sacrificed myself for you so that you could be born.

I whistled at that. No holds were barred in this fight to win back the wandering boy from the errors of Princeton to the good old American values of one per cent of the population.

"When did you get your notice to quit?"

"Yesterday. Just before my last exam. That didn't help either, although I think I'll pass. Not that it will matter now. Dad said I was through, so far as he was concerned. He'd waste no more of his money on me. My letter was the last straw."

"Last straw? How come?"

The undergraduate moved shyly in his chair, and smiled pathetically in his effort to hold back his tears.

"I told Dad I was not going to major in physics as he had wanted me to. I was going to major in history because I'm planning to become a minister."

"Didn't that please him?"

"Not on your life. He said that no son of his would ever become a minister. A minister is just a kept man living on the charity of others. My wanting to be a minister convinced him that I was a 'Nigra' lover at heart, and that I couldn't be changed. He would, therefore, waste his money on me no longer."

"So that's it? That doesn't mean you'll have to leave. The headmistress of a primary school phoned me this morning to ask if I could find someone to teach games to her first- and second-grade boys. You're the man for that job. Next, I'll phone Brad Craig of the Bureau of Student Aid. I'm sure he'll work out some kind of scholarship for you. We can't let you go just because of money. Your education is just beginning. Let Princeton complete what it began."

He stayed. He graduated. He is in the ministry. The university had been, for him, the place where he experienced his freedom.

If the backward-looking mood was inhibiting, I'm not sure that the forward look was much better. That too had its disadvantages. What passed as hope was simply a naïve belief that good old Yankee know-how, science, and the dollar would make everything all right—for the U.S.A. if not for anyone else. Middle-class morality and middle-class efficiency would triumph. This meant that a middle-class utopia would be created for everyone to enter who knew the password. This was the faith that had to be kept. This was the hope. Science and technology were the means. The Christian faith was merely a piece of window dressing.

The good future was assured because of a right approach to operant behavior. Professors of behavioral engineering and conditioning techniques were all that were required; students hardly, and religion not at all. The future lay on the drawing boards of experts in politics, sociology, psychology, and education. That may be a good thing, but many academic people forgot that students live now, not in the utopia that never is.

For the campus this meant that undergraduates were regarded as brains to be processed. One friend of mine maintained that the university existed only for the brain. I pointed out that I had never yet seen a brain without a body. He was not amused.

What I had to preach and what the campus as a whole was saying were in conflict. I said, "What counts for you as human beings is the great debate about existence, human destiny, suffering, sin, salvation, faith, hope, love, freedom, truth, man, God."

But the campus said, "That great debate doesn't count for grades, for promotion, for tenure, or for government contracts. It is too nonintellectual, too nonrewarding, too embarrassingly personal. What pays off are the facts which can be observed, and the methods which can be used. What doesn't are the inner life, reflection, conviction, commitment, and God. The great debate asks the kind of questions that cannot be answered precisely, therefore, why ask them?"

The campus itself was a kind of utopia, a no-place, where feelings were not expected to be expressed, and where a gulf existed between those who knew and those who didn't. In other words, there was a student-faculty hiatus, and only the undergraduates knew it.

One evening when I was driving back from Newark Airport I picked up a student. He was very grateful. We had an hour of sincere conversation. As we drove into Princeton he said, "I've enjoyed this. I once had a ride from Professor X. I told him how much undergraduates liked to talk with professors. Do you know what he told me?" My guest had obviously been shocked by it.

"No, tell me."

" 'Have you never thought that the faculty may not be particularly interested in talking with you? We've got our research, our papers to write, our committees to attend, our lectures to prepare. Whatever time we have left over we can use more profitably than speaking to students.' "

"But that is an extreme view surely? Not all faculty members feel that way."

"No, not all. But not too many feel the other way. Those who do are swamped with requests. Here we are. Could you let me off at my club?"

I turned into Prospect Street and let him off.

So many of our attitudes encourage this division. That professor was only saying what advertisements, magazines, politicians, parents, and even preachers, were saying: "To be with it you must be a success. This is what really, really matters. Study hard, work hard, eat your spinach, and you'll be a success. If you are a success, everybody will love you. You'll get into a good college, you'll get a lovely wife, you'll be given a safe place in the city, and a house with a four-car garage in the suburbs."

Poor Jesus, he never made it. He failed. That's why he was crucified.

Although campus attitudes deified the brain and its realm of unfeeling and uncaring facts, and society deified success, both united in their condemnation of undergraduates because they were noninvolved, uncaring, quiet, and grade-seekers.

At a meeting of alumni, one alumnus of the thirties said that he was shocked by the indifference of contemporary undergraduates. A senior who was present replied,

"Yes, a lot of us are cool. But isn't that the way you want us? We work hard to get good grades. We don't take risks in case any mistakes will be marked on our records for the CIA or FBI or graduate school to see. Our courses aren't challenging us to think beyond ourselves, or to think of other people. Maybe we'll keep on playing it safe until someone on the campus shows us how to think more deeply, and to act less selfishly."

In saying this he admitted his sense of guilt as a member of a highly privileged twentieth-century group, and at the same time asked for guidance. His need is that of our time, for models of humanity, for men who live their faith.

These disadvantages did not depress me. They indicated that the campus is just as sinful as any society of men, and that its need of God's grace is just as great. This was the situation I knew, and in which I felt at home.

If the times were against the Gospel, they were also for it. The big campus issue at the time I came was the Father Halton controversy. He was a Dominican priest who was chaplain to Roman Catholic students. His financial support came from an autonomous group, the Aquinas Institute. He was a man with a sense of mission: that of reclaiming the campus for the true faith.

He moved into the focus of the campus vision by attacking an article in *The Atlantic*. It was written by Professor Walter Stace,* a distinguished philosopher and scholar of Hegel. The article predated those of the radical theologians. It was also more clearly expressed, and indicated that a substitute for religion was required for the twentieth century. Right or wrong, it was contemporary.

Father Halton presumed that Walter Stace spoke for the

* "Man against Darkness," Sept. 1948.

whole campus. He concluded that it discriminated against true learning and true religion. This was as good an opening broadside as any to initiate the debate. That debate never materialized. Instead, a series of monologues appeared. These dealt with academic freedom on the one side, and religious discrimination on the other. They moved from Stace's article to the department of religion, the caliber of the faculty, the Communist affiliation of the university, the treachery of Catholic faculty, the impotence of the Chapel, and the evil of the clubs.

Father Halton debated from too narrow a premise, and the campus from too broad a one. What disturbed me most was the lack of religious consciousness on the part of the campus spokesmen. The foundation of academic freedom is deeper and stronger than the free expression of opinion. It is faith in the freedom of God. On this faith the College of New Jersey was built in 1746. In 1956 we had forgotten.

Whatever the faults of Father Halton, he challenged us to be true to our profession, *Dei sub numine viget*. He also reminded us that "man cannot live by bread alone." The freedom of the spirit is often subordinated to the slavery of the dollar. One fund raiser was forced into the embarrassing position of upholding this tenet when he suggested that my support of Martin Luther King was detrimental to the wealth of the campus.

As a university we were free to learn from Father Halton's extremism. He went too far when he claimed that he was the only non-Communist member of the faculty at Princeton. He was not a member of the Princeton faculty, and Princeton professors are as American as anyone else. He merits, however, one last shot (it was also one of his last):

"It would be wrong to leave the impression that religious discrimination is common currency at Princeton. It would be unfair. I would know of no man in the past fifty years whose check was refused by the Princeton Fund because of his religious affiliation.

"If one gives generously to Princeton, one may violate all

the special graces, eat like a cannibal and dip a gloved hand into the martini to fetch the olive—and still be the life of the party on Prospect Street. [*This is the street of the eating clubs.*]

"And if, as a millionaire, when you are dying, you call not for a priest, but for the University Treasurer, the President himself may come along to administer the last rites and hold your hand—the one with the pen in it. If you give all that you possess he will send your soul on its way with a hymn—the trustees humming (contentedly by now) in the background. Then, they will close your eyes, blot the will, shake hands all round, have a drink and say: 'Well, who's next?' "

If Father Halton and the senior members of the university missed the opportunity of dialogue, it was taken up by the undergraduates. They realized that the debate should have centered upon the subject of faith. Discussion was open and healthy. Ears were still sensitive to what the Gospel had to say to men of the twentieth century. Christianity was a lively option.

In the fall of 1956, I invited Bryan Green, an English evangelist, to lead a university mission. We began with a dialogue sermon and continued through the week. Approximately five hundred attended every evening. After each lecture we moved to the Chapel for a brief epilogue. At least half followed him for the service. During the last epilogue he said,

"You all know what a sacrament is. It is the outward and visible sign of an inward and invisible grace. Life is a sacrament. Faith expresses itself in action. Love becomes bread and wine, housing and clothing for the needy. Christ was a sacrament. He was God in the flesh: spirit in tangible form. Some of you may wish to express your experience of God's grace. You may have come to a new understanding of him, or you may have decided to commit yourself to him more deeply than in the past. If you do, I suggest that you make a sacramental act. Here are some cards. Write your names on them. We'll have a period of silent prayer. After the benediction you may come up to the altar: Leave your card and go in peace."

About eighty climbed the chancel steps, walked through the long quire with its exquisitely carved wood, and placed their cards on the holy table. It was a quiet sacramental celebration of God's activity. It was also a demonstration of the openness of the campus to the Gospel.

I have leaned heavily on God's grace. That grace I believed to be mediated through many channels and people. The most effective of these were those of the faculty who have a witness to share. Repeatedly undergraduates have told me that the examples set by certain faculty members were the strongest influences in their lives. This was true of the humanities. It was also true of the sciences.

One graduate wrote to a favorite professor to say:

> The greatest asset that I gained as a geology major was faith. Here I learned about a world which has been sensibly, scientifically, and logically evolved over a period of two billion years. It seems to me that studying this panorama gives one a feeling of awe, humility, and reverence for the process of life. If all the top leaders of the world had to take such courses and participate in field trips, how could they for one moment contemplate the destructive policies they do? As nothing else in my life has done, this training has led me to religious faith.

With this kind of experience taking place on the campus, my work as a minister was possible. One parent wrote to say how much he was moved by his son's letter about a professor of chemistry, and enclosed a copy.

> His lecture on the substance of his course was perhaps the most eloquent I have ever heard at this university and probably the most disturbing. What he is pointing out is perfectly true: The things which made America what it is today, if they are not lacking, are certainly in less obvious abundance than they were previously. I hope that the old axiom "check a cloud and you'll find a silver lining" holds.

You can catch a glimpse of this silver lining here, now and then, but how people have changed. I really wonder if the type of person you find around here on campus could really develop into the good-old New England horse-sense type. It was interesting to hear the professor say all of what he did. It reminded me of someone who builds something and is dissatisfied with it, although it is an advancement. He is and has been a contributor to the technological revolution that has changed this nation.

This professor represented the absurdity of the old science-religion debate. He was a man of faith and a scientist. His emphasis was on being a man: for it is not the scientist who makes the man, but the man, the scientist. In one faculty discussion a group of humanists were complaining about the outdatedness of the Christian faith. The thesis they upheld was that faith cannot be verified by the scientific method. Because it cannot, it has nothing to contribute to man's knowledge of himself.

The scientists who were present kept quiet. At last one of them said, "Your discussion has been interesting, and your arguments almost convincing. You have given science a place of eminence. You have left out one very important factor, however, and that is man. I don't believe science has the last word about him. I'm a scientist, yes, but when I leave the lab and go home, I am a man, a husband, a father, a friend, a member of a church. It is not my scientific knowledge that characterizes me as a man. It is my relationship with others. I am less capable of talking about God than most of you, yet I have to say a word for him. God may get along without us extremely well, but I don't know that man can live without God and still be man. We are brothers by our faith and love."

That ended the discussion. It confirmed my estimate that the campus was still open to grace. Indeed the critical approach of the academic method was a two-edged sword. It may have discouraged some from engaging in a spiritual discipline, but it also failed to meet the demands of a man in search of himself.

One of the first undergraduates to visit me did so because he saw no point in continuing with his studies. They were meaningless and pointless. They were a game of which he was weary. He began by questioning the system which had taught him to question. He ended by committing himself as a follower of Jesus Christ.

In a conversation which included another student he remarked,

"Our trouble is: we don't have time for God. The work load is tough. At least it is for me. I'm kept so busy grinding away in the lab or at my books that I kid myself that the scholastic values are the only ones that count. This makes me skeptical about life in general. In a few years guys will be saying, 'If I spend any time on God I'll flunk out!' What happens is: we accept scholastic values without question in order to survive, then we discover that we've missed the real thing. This is where religion should fill the gap. I guess this is your chief problem: how do you present or 'sell' your remedy for this spiritual void?"

"Do you have any suggestions?"

"Not many. Maybe you can help Princeton men to find relief from their scholastic trials. One remedy is to have social get-togethers with women. But how the cause of religion can be served that way, I don't know. I believe the personal approach is the best. Christians on campus have something to sell, that includes hope, confidence, optimism. All we have is ourselves as samples. We must meet every freshman face to face in the same way that you are trying to do. That means we'll have to take the time to do what is really important."

I listened attentively. My education was continuing. I was learning that a large part of my time would be spent in listening. That was a fair exchange for my twenty minutes' worth of speaking on Sundays.

The criticism of the negatively critical approach to existence forced undergraduates to risk taking part in the great debate. There were occasions and events where and when their objectivity was challenged, and their humanity was left showing. The tragedy was that there is too little in our culture to reinforce this awareness of being human. Whatever their failings, I have been constantly indebted to writers such as Kafka, Hesse, Sartre, Camus, Beckett, and T. S. Eliot. They have helped to introduce many a man to himself. I believe their work is a form of prevenient grace. To show a man his place in the universe for what he is, not a king, but a beggar, is to prepare him for the gift of grace.

I was reminded that another ally in my work would be the creative arts. So long as they are sensitively human there is a possibility of honest debate on the ultimate issues. There is every likelihood that humanity began with religion and art rather than with technology and government. The artist and the prophet are more basic than the toolmaker and the warrior.

The biggest advantage of all was the students. It was through them that grace would operate. There were those who were hostile to faith, there were those who were indifferent, but there were those who were faithful. Because of them there was a witness to God.

On my way to my study a sophomore stopped me by the door of the Chapel.

"You've got to hear this. It is priceless."

"What?"

"In sociology the other day the lecturer asked, 'How many of you believe in the existence of God?' "

"How many?"

"There were thirteen of us. Only five said they did."

"Only five? I think that's great, particularly in sociology."

"I don't agree. I think it is terrible. That's less than half."

He said this with a note of perplexity. We were facing the sundial, a copy of the one at Corpus Christi college in Oxford. Its symbol is that of the resurrection, the assurance of the triumph of life in the face of death. I looked back from that timeless critic of time to the youthful student with the anxious face.

"I think that's great. Five out of thirteen? Marvelous. Do you realize what that means: 50/130, 500/1,300, 5,000/13,000, 50,000/130,000, 5,000,000/13,000,000? Believers are always in a minority. God stood alone before the world in Jesus. He left a handful to compete with Rome. Five out of thirteen? In these days it is a miracle of grace."

He looked at me in astonishment, questioning my sanity.

"I hadn't thought of it that way."

"Please do. There is no evidence to assume that God is the voice of the majority, or that he is on the side of the big battalions."

His look of concern changed to one of amusement.

"I believe you're right. Thank God for that. I've been too influenced by Dr. Gallup and his polls. I've been worrying so much about quantity that I've forgotten about quality. That doesn't come in a mass."

"With five out of thirteen we have people to work for, and through. We've got a show on the road. We're under way." And that, I thought, is by the grace of God.

There was yet another advantage in my favor: Princeton's tradition. Underneath her pride and folly there is a living memory which gives the university a personality. Like those of us who are its members, it has a soul. Men of faith made its existence possible, men of faith have kept it alive, men of faith will redeem it so that it will struggle to express God's will for its times.

As for me, I had to witness to the reality of the grace that makes authentic life possible.

4

GRACE has caught me by surprise. That is why I am alive, and a preacher. I could not minister to the campus unless I believed that God is active. I refuse to accept the blame for its sins or the responsibility for its salvation. These belong to God. He is boss. His shoulders are broad enough to bear the burden of its sins, and his heart big enough to give it the love it needs.

Perhaps I have been surprised by grace because I have known so much evil. My boyhood was in the depression. Whatever its causes, its consequences were devastating. My home was by the Firth of Clyde. Our back door faced the sea. Our front door faced the road. Hardly a night passed but two or three men knocked at the door for help. After a meal they were given a shakedown bed in the kitchen or hallway. They were destitute men searching desperately for work and dignity. Some were defeated by their poverty. Their bodies were pulled out of the water. Whoever found them telephoned the police from our house. The body lay on a bench by the front door, covered by a blanket my father kept for that pathetic purpose. Society paid for the cost of the funeral. That was the final irony.

The depression darkened into the nightmare of World War II, mud and blood, prison camp and the death house. This was my experience of the twentieth century. Yet in the darkness there was always a gleam of light, in the "dreichness" of evil there was always a touch of grace.

At the end of the war I visited a bomb-blitzed area of London. Most of the fallen masonry had been removed and the ruins of the slum tenements stood stark, dark, and tragic like blasted trees in a desert. It was a powerful picture of the wasteland as Salvador Dali might have painted it, or as T. S. Eliot has depicted it in words:

> A heap of broken images, where the sun beats,
> And the dead tree gives no shelter, the cricket no relief,
> And the dry stone no sound of water
> . . . [and] fear in a handful of dust.*

No theologian could have said more about the fall of man than those ruins. They screamed of despair. They wept black, sooty tears for the plight of humanity. "See," they sighed, "this is what you have done to brick and cement. Think of what you have done to flesh and blood."

It was our wasteland, all right. Yet, even here, there was hope. I glanced at the barren shell of what had been a damp, dingy basement. A sliver of sunshine slipped through a crack in the wall and shone upon a solitary dandelion, a golden weed growing bravely on a fragment of soil.

This touch of grace makes all the difference. It may be insufficient proof for a system of philosophy, but it puts bubbles into the champagne of life. I find that it is better to light a candle than to curse the darkness.

For the dogmatist my position is untenable. Yet for me, as a campus preacher, it is a point of departure for many a discussion. Theological and scientific dogmatism have been rejected. Its absolutism is feared by contemporary minds. I find myself closer to the position of Bertrand Russell as he has expressed

* From "Choruses from 'The Rock'" in *Collected Poems 1909–1962* by T. S. Eliot. Used by permission of Harcourt, Brace & World, Inc.

it: "Uncertainty, in the presence of vivid hopes and fears, is painful, but must be endured if we wish to live without the support of comforting fairy tales. It is not good either to forget the questions that philosophy asks, or to persuade ourselves that we have found indubitable answers to them. To teach how to live without certainty, and yet without being paralyzed by hesitation, is perhaps the chief thing that philosophy in our age can still do for those who study it."

I think Bertrand Russell is optimistic in his support of philosophy as a bridge between theology and science, at least as far as its present mood is concerned. His understanding, however, is similar to that of the man of faith.

Whoever says the last word cuts off discourse. The first word, I believe, is always with God. He is the initiator of dialogue. This I have found to be true on the campus.

I have been surprised by the willingness of some undergraduates to engage in discussion although they believed it impossible.

"I am not sure why I've come to talk to you," said one undergraduate, "but here I am."

"Why are you not sure?"

"Because the only point at which we can begin and end is in disagreement."

"Why are you so sure about that if you are so uncertain about everything else?"

"That's obvious. You believe in God. I don't. At least I'm not sure. You go in for this Jesus worship. I cannot. You believe in good and evil. I'm not sure. Because I'm not sure you are bound to believe that I'm lost."

"Am I? That's interesting news. I did not know that I had to believe you were lost. I have no idea of what purpose God has for you."

"But you are bound. We cannot agree with each other. If I agree with you, then I'll be wrong. If you agree with me you'll be wrong."

"Why?"

"Because you're religious and I'm not."

"You are not? I am? Yet we are both concerned about life. Are you sure you know which one of us is religious?"

"You are. What beliefs I have are inaccurate, so will be my future ones. My beliefs are in flux. When an experience does not fit into a rational pattern, I form a new belief."

"So? What's so great about that?"

"If your God has told you that all swans are white, you have to believe that. You cannot admit that some swans could be black?"

"Can't I? I thought I could."

"No. Your religious attitude prohibits you from modifying your belief about swans. You may say that if a bird is black it is not a swan. Or you may say it is really white but we don't see it that way."

"I'm not certain that I see the point you are making. Are you telling me that I am honor bound to accept a dogmatic view of the universe unrelated to the evidence, for example, that God created it Sunday through Friday and rested on Saturday?"

"Yes, or something like that. Religion cannot explain the world. Look at what people like you are trying to do to come to terms with Freud. Tillich has to bend over backward to explain man's cosmic loneliness in religious terms."

"You believe then that religion is dead. Scientific knowledge has replaced it and philosophy?"

"Yes. People cling to religious dogma only because it helps them to feel comfortable. They cannot be persuaded that their dogmatic beliefs are not right."

"That is true of lots of people who are not religious, as well as those who are. Are you not saying that man and his theories are not absolute? I would go along with that. I don't have the last word on anything. I don't know ultimate truth. Yet, as I say that, there is truth by which I live. There is a clue to existence, which faith provides. I'd be a fool not to work with it."

"I don't believe in faith."

"You don't. What do you believe in?"

"I suppose I have to say that I believe in uncertainty. The world contains so many things about which I'm not certain. The attempt to understand these things is exciting. The adventures of a mountain climber will end when he grows old, but for me there is no end. All life holds adventure upon adventure. I must engage in an adventure with something 'because it is there.' "

"And you believe religion prevents that kind of adventure?"

"Yes, I do."

"I'm sorry about that. Religion has done a bad job. I can see why you insist that we must disagree. I would not wish to violate that disagreement. The God that Jesus has taught me to trust, cannot be defined, neither can his ways. He is eternal. That means endless. Infinitely open. The man of faith is the man who follows him not knowing where. Keep reminding me that there is no certainty; there are only frontiers."

That lad was right to reject the authoritarianism of the old infallible position of the dogmatist. Rules are never enough. Where we begin is with our fallibility as men and nations. Our best is not the answer. We never arrive at perfection. We're always on the way. We have no certainty. Perhaps the miracle of life is that we respond to uncertainty. That in itself is an act of grace.

My certainties have never worked out. Before World War II, I received an appointment from the Colonial Office to Malaya. I declined it, not because I was uninterested, but because I was certain that a war was on its way and that it would be fought in Europe. I turned from the Colonial Service to the army and ended up in Malaya.

I was certain that I would find my lifework in some so-called underprivileged area of the world. Here I am in Princeton, embarrassed by its affluence.

I was certain at one time that reason was the answer to all human problems, yet here I am preaching on faith, and dependent on grace.

I was certain that a college religious program could be planned and executed. I have learned to expect the unexpected and to use it for the glory of God.

When I took up my campus ministry I arranged several meetings with faculty and students in order to find ways of cooperating in projects such as drama, the creative arts, and conferences. The majority opinion was that nothing could be done. No one was interested. I approached a foundation with a series of sparkling ideas only to be told that the foundation would consider giving me support once I had demonstrated the success of these ideas. That was something I could not do without money.

I tried all the sources of expertise that I knew. Nothing happened. One day the chairman of the Chapel deacons asked,

"Do you mind if we put on a play in the chancel?"

"Mind? Mind? I've been suggesting something like that for the past three years. What do you propose?"

"*Everyman Today!* It is an up-to-date version of the old morality play. John Stang estimates that he can do the lighting for under eighty dollars. He has it all figured out. The symbolism can be highlighted effectively to demonstrate change of moods. It will be theater in the square."

It was. It has continued for the past ten years. The productions include *Don Juan in Hell, Dr. Faustus, The Sign of Jonah, The Brothers Karamazov, A Sleep of Prisoners, The Prisoner, J.B., A Man for All Seasons, The Easter Maastrich Play, The Flag* by Bink Noll.

I had planned to have a series of nightly organ and musical meditations. The experts told me that there were not enough organists and that a "hi-fi" system would be unsuitable.

On the last night of *Everyman Today*, one of the deacons came into my study.

"Why don't we keep the Chapel open until midnight? During the rehearsals guys have been dropping in on their way back from the library. They've watched rehearsals, and stayed to listen to the organ."

"That's all very well once in a while. We couldn't do it every night."

"Oh yes we could. I've got enough organists lined up. How about having the organ begin about eleven, and go on to past midnight?"

"Fine. We'll advertise it as the nightly organ Epilogue, and raise the extra money to pay for the night watchmen."

A freshman suggested a coffee break after the Sunday morning service. So we have a coffee break. The same has been true of study and discussion groups, and social service projects. These occasions which make eventful meeting between people possible have resulted from uncertain or haphazard situations, rather than from planned ones. From this, I learned of the need to trust both God and people: for out of such trust arises that spontaneity so essential to authentic human life.

More than that: I learned of the deep need in the hearts of some undergraduates for God's love. They were conscious that the context of their lives was greater than that of home, society, and university. In their way, they sought that city, "whose architect and builder is God."

At one of my lunchtime discussion groups, the subject of dogmatic agnosticism arose. A junior described his position:

"When I came here as a freshman, I was sure that religion was for the birds. I saw all the answers to life in purely objective terms. I loved theories—boy, did I love them. What I didn't know was that I wasn't in the position to make the final verdict about the universe. That was what I was doing. I was the cool observer and judge of life. Everything was wrong but me. I didn't need any help. Getting into Princeton was the big deal for me. This was what I wanted. Now I was on my way to knowledge. The more I knew, the better I would become. But that didn't work out. I became less certain that there was an answer to everything."

Another student broke in:

"Do you mean to say that you lost faith in your disbelief?"

"Yes, I did."

"That has happened to me too. I thought everything was black and white. The professors could give a black-and-white answer, and I'd have no doubts. Now I have lots of doubts. Most of them are about myself, and about my former certainties. What helped you?"

"A lit. course. I started discussing T. S. Eliot with a roommate. The Waste Land and "The Hollow Men" gave me a good description of what I was beginning to feel about life in general. Then the "Choruses from 'The Rock'" and Ash Wednesday made me think that there was an awful lot more to life than concepts and propositions. I discovered the dimension of faith. I started dropping into the organ epilogues. Next I came to the services. I hadn't been in church since I was nine. Now I'm getting a lot out of it."

This is typical of the unexpected that keeps happening.

For a while I had the pleasure of precepting in psychology. After an evening precept,* a senior asked,

"May I stay behind and talk with you?"

I looked at him and wondered what he could possibly want to speak to me about. He was a tall, blond, athletic young man with that air of confidence which seems to be purchased in elegantly wrapped packages from Brooks Brothers and Abercrombie and Fitch. He looked too grand for my shabby living room.

Before he sat down he blurted out, "How can you teach psychology and still believe in God?"

That stumped me. I kept talking until I could think of something to say. Eventually, I heard myself saying,

"I don't have to stop believing in order to precept in psychology."

"But psychology is all about environmental conditioning and techniques of behavioral engineering."

"I think there is more to it than that. I don't have to agree with every theory we discuss. I hope I leave them open to criticism. But you don't want a lecture on that. What's bugging you?"

* A cross between a tutorial and a seminar.

"I think psychology is one of the conditioning gadgets of our time. It is a device to turn us against God. Everything in society conditions us against him."

I could see that there was something on his heart that was hidden by his words. He was talking until he could say it, like myself.

"I see what you mean. Yes, our whole environment conditions us against God. We presume that we are mature, that we have come of age, that we can run the whole show by means of machinery, politics, slogans, and money."

"We do, we surely do. We kid ourselves. We are phoneys. As I've figured it out, we are encouraged by society and schools to live by the double standard. To think one thing and do another. We think we're good. We're not. Our lives are really rotten."

Now, I thought, he's coming to the point.

"I don't think that is the whole picture," I said. "We are only half-rotten, half-good. We're a pinch of dust, but we're also a pinch of dreams."

"But when you come down to it, the dust dominates. Look at us here in Princeton. We think we're the greatest. Our education encourages us to be independent, to be on our own intellectually. We develop a kind of intellectual egotism. What does that do for us? It results in unbearable loneliness. We are taught to be proud. We bow before no one. To acknowledge God would result in a loss of this intellectual snobbery. It would make us humble. That's bad for our image.

"Another thing is that we're separated from life. The ivory tower is a dream world. We create problems that do not exist and then solve them. That makes us feel good. We become intellectual heroes. If that isn't play-acting, I don't know what is."

I nodded my head in agreement. He had a lot on his heart. He continued:

"Take me. I swallowed this gook. I thought I was sophisticated. The cool type who knew what he was doing. I have a red sports car. I'm a seducer of women. I've got it all worked out."

"But you know you haven't. What pricked the balloon?"

"First of all, a sermon of yours."

"That surprises me. So often I feel that I've hit the same old nail on the head, or spoken into a vacuum."

"That sermon hit me. It was the first one in my freshman year. You left me with an uncertain feeling about everything. You pulled me up with a jerk. I felt angry with you. My safe world had gone."

I thought I had better not pursue this subject: for I couldn't remember the sermon. I switched.

"What's the next pinpoint?"

"My father."

"Your father? How come?"

"He's the big Princeton type. *The Success!* I'd grown up to believe that he was everything. God wasn't needed with him around. He was the tower of strength. Master of the home, lord of the community, paradigm of the virtues."

As he said this there was a bitterness in his voice. The model of morality must have been shattered.

"You know what he is. He is a phony. He's had a mistress for years. I thought my mother was the weak one of the family. She isn't. He's a blob of jelly. She came down with him to see me this morning. Or rather, she brought him down. She wanted him to tell me face to face that he's getting a divorce. So that's the end of that."

"End of what?"

"End of a lot of things, I guess."

"But not the end of you."

"No, I don't think so. It's the end of the double standard as far as I'm concerned. My mother was the real person. Thank God I've learned that lesson. She knew about him for years, but she put up with him for the sake of my sister and myself."

"She sounds like quite a woman."

"She is. And there is another one."

"Is there? Who is she?"

"I met this girl. I liked her, and I tried to make her. She wasn't having anything. She told me her views. They're good. That helped me to understand that it was she I was falling in love with, and not only sex. Now I love her very much."

"You sound as though you've got a lot going for you. You're probably closer to life than you've ever been. There's one thing, however, you needn't do."

"What's that?"

"Hate your father! You've seen that he's lived only by the convenient conventions of our society. Help him to see that too. If you want you can let your bitterness make you a phoney. Remember you've got your mother and your girlfriend to help you. What's he got?"

"Not much. Maybe a bag of wind, and a sense of guilt."

"And that's a pretty thin gruel, isn't it?"

"It is. As you say, I've got something to go on. It is up to me. Maybe that is the beginning of growing up."

The popular opinion of churchly circles decrees that young people lose their faith when they go to college. This may be true in some instances. I have found, however, that it is often upperclassmen who become sincerely interested in the religious dimension of life. The reasons are many. It may be because of a family situation, a critical analysis of conventional values, or an openness to think honestly about religion. Shortly before his graduation one senior said,

"It was only in my senior year that I learned through actual experience how important religion is. A number of living experiences—one of these was the death of my best friend—have corroborarted the knowledge I had gained from my reading. I believe that this new awareness will make me study the Bible."

Another senior came crashing into my study. He was tall, with a long freckled face. He was impatient.

"Tell me something? Do you think there is a purpose to life? I'm not quite sure what I mean, but I guess that's the brunt of my question."

"Of course I do. I wouldn't be here if I didn't. What's on your mind?"

"This sounds funny. I know it does."

"I cannot know that until you tell me. What is it?"

"I'm graduating with highest honors, Sigma Xi, and one of the top fellowships for grad school. When I say it, it sounds great. I've achieved everything I've ever dreamed of. This is what is funny. It means nothing to me. I thought that this was what counted. Once I made it I would be somewhere. But I'm not. I'm the same. The only difference is that now I don't know where I'm going. I don't know what it's all about. You're a man of faith. Tell me."

That's a tall order for anyone. It is easy to criticize what someone else has said or written about his faith. It is another to describe these insights, experiences, and thoughts which have formed your own. I gave him a brief summing up of what I believed about man as a conscious being; of creation and man's place in it; of faith as a man's response to God's initiative; of life in the community of faith.

When I had finished he said,

"That sounds pretty good to me. It makes sense. Guess I'd better get involved in some church or other, else I'll run out of steam."

Within a day or two he sent his roommate for a similar conversation.

One of the most unexpected of discussions began with a telephone call.

"You probably don't remember me. I sat beside you at a Princeton Today dinner about a month ago. There is something I have to talk to you about. I'm coming down to Princeton tomorrow. May I look in to see you?"

I wondered what he had to talk about. I had been on my best behavior for some time, and I had not said anything rude to him at the dinner.

Next day he knocked at my door. I remembered him. We had talked about some of the great yacht designers, and some of the old sailing ships. Now he wanted to talk about himself. His university days had meant a great deal to him. He had majored in mathematics, and had maintained his interest in the subject. This continuing study gave him much intellectual satisfaction, and kept him interested in the university. He was head of a business, and had worked hard to get that. In fact, he had worked so hard that he never stopped to reflect on the nature of his life. Suddenly he found himself with nothing.

"I was on the brink of a black abyss. It made me want to panic. What do you do when you are fifty-two, and you find that you've been working so hard that you've lost yourself?"

"Don't panic. Sit down and find out where you are. When I was on reconnaissance in the jungle once I passed through an area of lodestone. My compass was no good. I was tempted to press on in the direction of where I believed my destination to be. I didn't. I sat down and looked. The leaves of some of the trees were pressed one way. That meant east. The prevailing wind was from the west. I checked north with my watch against the sun. I saw that the stream flowed approximately southeast. It would flow into a river. Somewhere along the river there would be a village. You needn't be lost if you pause to reflect."

"That's what I've started to do. That's why I came back here. Princeton has meant so much to me. This is where I'll begin to find my way. It has given me a great deal intellectually. I believe it can help me spiritually. So I've come to you. The Chapel suggests the answer. Now what do I do?"

"Look a bit further. Buy yourself a *New English Bible*. Read the New Testament. Don't read what someone says about it. Read it. See it in human terms. Hear what it is saying to you today. Take time to be quiet. Shut the door on the world. Let your memories of good direct your thinking. Remember who you are by remembering whose you are. You are God's. By God you are loved. You are, therefore, someone; someone who is lovable. Because you are, you can love. Remember too that there are others in the same boat as yourself. Seek them out.

Form a fellowship. Share your uncertainties with them. Share theirs. Read some of the great spiritual odysseys together, *Pilgrim's Progress*, Thomas Kelly's *Testament of Devotion*, *Cloud of Unknowing*, *John of the Cross*, MacNeil Dixon's *The Human Situation*, Brunner's *Credo*. There is plenty to keep you going."

"All right, I'll do that. I've got to become involved in the spiritual side of life. That I know. I know it within myself. Do you mind if I check with you from time to time? I'm liable to become confused."

He has checked with me. In doing so he has helped me. He has passed on suggestions about books, and about subjects for discussion. He has taken the measure of himself as a fragment of dust in the vast scale of cosmic space and time. He has also seen himself as a conscious being, as a man into whom God has breathed his life.

Perhaps he found that although for a time he had forgotten God, God had not forgotten him. Because he does not forget, God teaches us with grace to help us remember.

One Monday morning an undergraduate came into my study. He was smiling. The brightness of his intelligent face told me that he had news that had excited him.

"The darndest thing happened last night. I was coming back from New Haven. My head must have been in the clouds, for I missed the Garden State exit 14A. I went southbound on the Palisades at exit 13. My gas tank was empty so I got off at Orangeburg. Then I got lost looking for a gas station. I hadn't a clue where I was. I drove all around on those windy little roads. I'd stop and ask someone. All I got was bad advice that took me nowhere. I even followed another car past a detour sign. We went right up to a blockade. Between the bad advice, the dead end, and the empty tank, I was frantic."

"I can imagine you must have been. You were up the well-known creek without a paddle. How did you square things away?"

"I drove along slowly to save the little gas I had left. Then

I came upon a Dominican college. I don't know where it is. I could never find it again. I started to pull into the drive. But the place seemed empty. So I backed out. Then I saw a station wagon turn on its lights. I drove in quickly to catch it, and jumped out of the car. It was like a Bergman movie. I didn't have my coat on and it was cold. A nun got out of the car to see what I wanted. She could have thought I was demented, but she showed no sign if she did. I told her that I was lost, and out of gas. She went off to find help. First of all she checked with the head nun to see if I could get some gas from their pump. I could. Then she looked for the mechanic, but he was away. She took me to the pump, but it was locked."

"Did you see that as a parable of the Church's inability to fill the empty gas tanks of your generation?"

"Not quite: for the nuns led me to a gas station that was open. I filled up. Then they put me on the right road back to school. I figured that if the Church couldn't fill me up directly, it could lead me to where I could. And that it could put me on the right road. I've been thinking of that. I couldn't miss the parable. That's me, all right; out of gas, and at a dead end. I'm going to start listening to you from now on. You can help me fill up, and find my way."

"Thanks, chum! I'll give it a try."

My ministry has been outside the bounds of the institutional church. It has happened that way because the means of grace have never been limited to the machinery of ecclesiastical organization. When I came to ordination the committee in charge of this serious business was shocked to find that I did not have a record of a regular church membership. It was also shocked by my very broad interpretation of the church. I was classified as a bad risk, and as the candidate least likely to succeed.

To be true to experience, I could not deny that God's activity is much broader and deeper than his church recognizes it to be.

When I was at Hartford Seminary I needed money to pay my bills. I tried writing articles for magazines. I thought church people would be interested in what God had done in prison camp. I wrote an article on the subject. But where to send it was a problem. I decided on the *Christian Century* for two reasons. One, because it claimed to be Christian, and I believed that my experiences had been Christian. Second, prison camps are a regrettable factor in our twentieth century, and therefore have to be taken into account. My manuscript was rejected. The editor pointed out that I lacked the sociological evidence to make my story credible. I tore up my manuscript.

I returned to the United States shortly after Korea. There was a lot of fuss about the poor conduct of G.I.s in the prison camps. I wrote an article entitled "Lessons from Captivity" and sent it to *The Presbyterian Life*. It was rejected. The editor comforted me by telling me that he would accept an article on Main Street, U.S.A. but not about war or prisoners. His readers were not interested.

That's that, I thought, and used the manuscript to light the fire.

In a lecture I gave to a psychology class I used illustrations from my experience. About a week later I received a telephone call from one of the senior editors of *Reader's Digest*. "A son of one of our executives is at Princeton. He heard your lecture. He told us that you have a good story. Do you mind if I visit with you and write it up?"

"Not at all. Come down and give it a try."

He did. It was published as "Miracle on the River Kwai." One of the editors of Harper & Row said, "We think you have a story. Write us a book." I did. It was called *Through the Valley of the Kwai*. The worldly papers reviewed it kindly. The reviews of some church magazines indicated that I was theologically unsound. My formulas were wrong.

One such review pointed out that I had a good story, but that I did not know how to tell it. He disposed of me as an author. Then he did the same thing to me as a theologian: "The reader of this book will find out more about how to operate a little sailboat than he will about how God works in the human soul."

That put my gas to a peep. He is right. I know a little about a sailboat, but infinitely less about God. I had become a minister on the daring assumption that I could suggest to some people that God is still active in his crazy old world. I had studied some of the theological masters to help me in my task. I realized that none had a foolproof answer nor a leakproof formula. If they had, the world would have been saved, and amateurs like myself could stay safely with their boats or farms or factories.

The reviewer is in the same boat as myself. His criticism implied that he and his ecclesiastical organization had the last word about God. Because they had, they had earned the right to fence it around with their own manufactured safeguards. Too bad for them that God has not accepted their conclusion. He breaks through the flimsy barriers of theological propositions, and through the restricting walls of religious establishments. He is too big, and too free to be held in check. The professionals are usually unwilling to recognize this. That is why God is left to choose amateurs.

When God spoke to Israel in the eighth century B.C., it was through amateurs like Amos. He was denounced by the priest of Bethel because he was only a peasant. Amos justified his position by pointing out that although he was not a prophet nor a prophet's son, God had spoken to him.

When Jesus walked in Galilee it was not with experts, but with men. They knew more about sailboats, nets, and fish than they knew about the forms and formulas of religion. For me this is good news. I am one of these doubting Thomases who do not take for granted what the experts tell them. Whatever truth is, it has to be mine. I have to say "Yes" to it with my own lips and mind. It must be a part of what I am.

There are many like me. We are not naturally obedient. We are unwilling to be controlled, told, or pushed around. We claim the freedom to be what we are, and to suffer for it. We cannot sum up truth in a formula. All we can do is to live it the best we can. We cannot say as the Fascists, or Communists, or Fundamentalists do, "Here is the truth in my theory of race, society, or God." Because we cannot, we are left standing somewhere between the dark and the dawn. With my brethren I stand in the chill of this grayness, and wait patiently for the day.

During a summer vacation I received a letter from an undergraduate, in which he wrote:

> I cannot put an address on this letter. I do not know where I am. You are familiar with this situation, for you have heard me speak of it often enough. I crossed some mountains, then a river. Now I am sitting in my car on a dirt road. I am on the plain. The land stretches out to join the sky. There are tall trees behind me. It is dark. Yet in a funny sort of way it is light. Light enough to see by. Where the light is coming from I do not know. I know it only by its action. The sky is silver and the clouds are blue. They seem to have exchanged color at this place and at this time. I do not know where I am. Yet I do. I'm just to the left of the evening star. When you read this you will think that this is a good place for me to be.

He was right. To the left of the evening star is not a bad place to be. It describes the human situation. It is, therefore, one of hope. We can always take a bearing on a star.

There have been moments when the mystery of grace has opened me to dimensions that are beyond articulation or comprehension.

During the war the only information my parents received was that I had probably been killed by enemy action while fleeing from the Japanese. My aunt said, "It isn't true. I see him surrounded by tall trees. He is alive." That same aunt got up at 5:30 A.M. one morning to cook a breakfast for a guest. Why? She did not know. She had to do it. That was all. She had fried an egg and a rasher of bacon. The tea was masking under a cozy. She was making the toast. There was a sharp knock at the door. She opened it. My brother stood there. He had been left behind at Narvick at the end of the ·niserable Norwegian campaign some months previously. The Norwegian underground had taken care of him. They shipped him out in a fishing boat. He was picked up by a patrol ship of the Royal Navy and taken to the naval base at Greenock where my aunt lived.

A fellow prisoner had cerebral malaria. That means curtains for most people. His situation was hopeless. He was in that fevered world between death and life, darkness and light, when suddenly he was aware of a brilliant light. The light became a sign which read, "The Lord is on your right hand, you will not fail." The fever left him. His tortured dreams disappeared. He was at peace.

"When I woke up next morning," he told me, "I knew I was going to live. I could still see these shining letters. They were like neon lights. I can't explain them. I've tried. Was this a text I'd heard my mother repeat when I was a child? Was it something I'd read? Whatever it was, it came to me at the last moment of life. Something happened and I'm alive. I can never forget. It turned me from death. Because of it, life has been different."

I told this story to a friend of mine in Sweden, who said, "That's funny. I know of a similar experience. I worked for the International Red Cross during the war. My task was to inspect prison and internment camps. At a German camp I met a girl of about twenty. I asked her how she was getting on. After a fairly general conversation she asked me if I would mind listening to an experience that had perplexed her. She had been captured on the eastern front along with a group of men who were freedom fighters. They were all condemned to death. On the evening before the execution a shining presence stood with her in the cell. She was calmed by the certitude that whatever happened she was in God's hands. At dawn she was taken out into the square and blindfolded along with the others. The officer gave his orders preparatory to firing. Suddenly an orderly rushed up to the officer with a message. The girl was released. The others were killed. Why she had been selected for mercy she did not know, and she could not understand."

"When you met the girl, how did she appear to you?"

"She was very intelligent. She was perplexed because she could not explain this incident. I cannot either."

He is now a professor of sociology at an American university.

Laurens van der Post, a South African author of note, had a similar experience. He was captured by the Japanese and informed that his head would be cut off in the morning. He dreamed that he saw his mother as a young girl. She knelt by a fountain along with a Bushman. Both cupped their hands and offered him water. His mother told him that it was the beginning. He woke up convinced that he would live.*

The same quality of mystery is known in less dramatic circumstances. On a Sunday evening I received a telephone call. "I'm in the hospital under sedation. I'd like to see you."

Within ten minutes I was in the ward. My caller was a student. He was excited; excited in the way a man is when he has made a fascinating discovery. He kept pacing up and down his room as he spoke to me.

"Sit down. I've a long story to tell. I was at a conference. I went out of curiosity, and also out of a sense of loneliness. My loneliness was that of desperation. I didn't think I could go on living. Life for me has been a series of circles: home, school, society. Each one kept me imprisoned. Sure, they were pretty prisons, but they were prisons. They were becoming so tight that I was suffocating. I felt that I was dying inside, and no one cared. I gave up trying to operate in these neat little circles. I despaired of them. The more I despaired the less controlling these circles became.

"It was in that state I went to the conference. I met a girl. I talked to her about my feelings. She understood. My experience was U-shaped. I came spinning down through these circles,

* Laurens van der Post, *The Lost World of the Kalahari* (New York: William Morrow, Apollo Edition), pp. 61, 62.

down to the bottom of the U. I was nothing, just a polished circle like the others. I confessed that. I went home completely dazed. Nothing was the same. The whole world was trembling. That night I felt terrible. A miracle happened. Suddenly I was free. I was full of life. I was breathing deep gulps of pure air. My home was no longer dark and oppressive, it was full of light. I could see things I had never seen before. I shot up to the top of the U."

He stopped pacing up and down, turned to me, and asked, "Have I made myself clear so far?"

"You have indeed. Go on."

"It's all so confusing. I told my parents about it. They took me to the doctor who gave me some pills to keep me quiet. They brought me down here so that I could be under observation. But I've never felt better, nor more certain about life. They don't understand that I am free, free at last. I'm free because of love. Love is life. It is the power that smashes your hard circle, strips you of your pride and leaves you a naked human being. Yes, naked, but a human being. That naked human being is what I'm ready to give, and to give up. I'm willing to give it to other people and to the world."

I was concerned about his burning enthusiasm, but interested in his logical and vivid interpretation. He looked at me with his clear eyes.

"Now I know what life is all about. Love is the power of life that leads you home to where you've always been, and always wanted to be, but you didn't know it. When you know you are loved, you are free to love, to love the world. I have a sense of being complete, of being a whole man, not pieces of one. I realize that love is everything. When you love, you don't need to have things: for you know how to be."

I was listening to him with my heart as well as my mind. At first I was suspicious. Hospital, drugs, elation, suggested a breakdown. Then I realized that if he were crazy, so was I, with the craziness the world needs for its salvation. I listened more carefully.

"I see everything so clearly. I was full of despair because I couldn't be what everyone wanted me to be. Oh sure, I was the bright boy who smiled sweetly, and who operated successfully, but I was never me. I was desperate because the world is hating itself to death. Violence, prejudice, greed, fear, that's all I could see in the world. Everything was chaos. Now I see the order that love brings to it. I see myself. I see through the absurdity of what is counted as reality, and I see the truth. I see the kingdom of God. I see that God is love. It doesn't matter what you call him. You don't need to call him anything. You can call him love: for that is what he is."

When he finished we shook hands. We stood together in silence for a moment or two. Then I left.

Next day I had a long conversation with his psychiatrist whom I knew. I related my experience, and expressed my uncertainties. I was told,

"I've seen him, and I am convinced that there is nothing seriously wrong with him. His sense of elation is unlike that of a schizophrenic or a manic depressive. He is clear and rational. Frankly I was stumped until I remembered what happened at the campfire meetings of the old revival days. I think he has an authentic experience of conversion. He is turned toward life. I think you can be of more help to him than I."

When I face the deeply personal or spiritual issues of existence, I am left without any answers. I do not know. That is the confession I am compelled to make. Meaning, grace, mystery, are beyond me, always beyond me. I do not complain. The wind blows where it will. The important thing is that it blows. If you are an exhausted, sweat-drenched little traveler in a desert, you do not deny the reality of the wind. Remember, an analysis of the meteorological conditions of your area will not help you. The wind will. When it blows, you stand up tall to let it blow through your sweaty rags or your Brooks Brothers suit. If you are a sailor and at sea, you trim your sheets and set a course for port.

5

I EXPECTED that sex would be an issue on campus. I never expected to find, however, that so many people would act as though it had just been discovered. They had forgotten that it has been with us since Eve. It is an integral part of human experience. One of the problems about it, which society has handed on to the young, is that it has been spoiled by the "cutting-up-people game." This is a game we all play. When we cut up a person into mind, body, emotions, and sex, we no longer see the person. We see only the bits and pieces lying on the table like a dissected frog.

Sex abstracted from men and women, and advertised as a commodity, has contributed to the mess-up of many a life.

"I'm leaving the university," said a junior to me.

"Why?"

"Because I'm fed up. There's nothing but work. No fun."

"But you needn't work all the time. You can have fun sometime, surely?"

"Not often enough. I like dates, but there aren't any here. It costs too much to bring them down. At weekends I'm bored."

"Don't you read books, go to the theater or the movies?"

"Have you read a book, or seen a movie recently that wasn't on sex?"

I admitted that I had not.

"Then what do you think it does to someone like me? It waves it in my face. It tells me to go out and find a hunk of it. Soon, we'll be able to buy it by the pound. That's the way it's dished up. I don't want to think of it that way. I'm going to a co-ed campus in the west. I want to meet with girls, not dream of sex."

"Do you think that will help you?"

"Yes, I do. I might even find a girl who is interested in the same things as me, or in the same courses. I'm sure I shall. It will be fun talking things over with her."

He was a victim of the sex-is-a-fun-thing-and-sells-cars attitude. He knew better than to be overcome by it. The wishy-washy nature of contemporary sexual morality, or no-morality, may be a reaction to the old morality of legal virtue and double standards. I know that the old morality was meant as a system of guidance and as a means of protection. Sex, however, became equated with sin. So long as a woman kept her virginity outside of marriage, she was a good woman. Once she lost it, she was branded as fallen. She was condemned. The old morality became destructive. The present practice of the deification of an organic function, however, may prove to be as equally destructive.

Young men often know what to do about sex, but not what to do about love. Sex education at home and school is fine. We should know as much about our bodies as we can. Sex education, good as it may be, cannot, however, take the place of education in love.

As young officers our standing order of the night was: "Seduction if possible, rape if necessary, but fornication at all cost." I am not sure that present attitudes are better or worse. Probably they are about the same. There are those who live by the sex-is-fun-and-that-is-all-that-matters rule. These are the young gentlemen who invite a young lady for a campus weekend. Their approach is simple, and therefore has the value of being direct: "Sleep with me, or go back where you came from." Some go back.

One young gentleman, well connected as those of an earlier generation used to say, and proud of his hard-polished shell of sophistication, asked a young lady to a prom weekend. During the dance he said, "This is pretty dull. A few friends are having a party at a motel on Route One. What you say we join them?" Someone should have told the girl about approach number one, but no one had. She said, "Okay. Let's."

They all went in a group. At the motel the couples went off into rooms. It was a number of parties for two. The girl said, "No." The boy said, "Good-by." The girl called her dad, who came at the double from a distance. The boy thought it was funny.

Some do not go back. To do so would be to lose face. They prefer to become slaves to the sex cult.

I was visiting the infirmary. A senior asked me to sit down for a chat. He discussed an article which had appeared in a magazine. Its general theme was the guidance of good taste.

"It makes sense to me," he said, laying his magazine down on the bedcover. "What do you think of it?"

"I've read it. It makes sense to me too. Often there aren't clear-cut lines separating the good from the bad. It is hard to know when the good leaves off and the bad begins. Most human problems cannot be solved by law. I don't know why we keep on thinking they should. Ready-made rules don't apply to every situation or apply to everyone. The article was dealing with the difficulty judges have in making judgments in what is pornography, and what is not. If we could encourage people to develop a sense of good taste, and to act accordingly, we'd do well. Maybe good sense is uncommon sense, or a sense of what is right or fitting. In that case it may mean a taste for the good."

The senior nodded his head sympathetically.

"I go along with the author. What is important is that we

make up our own minds. I guess that is what freedom is. I used to think that the thing to do was to be with it, that is, to go along with the other guys. I don't think that any more. I'm developing a sense of good taste, or a taste for the good. Some things are right for me, and some wrong. The judgments that count are my own. You won't believe this, but it is true."

"What is?"

"I've been telling some of the dates who come down here that they don't have to sleep around like girls in a Swedish movie."

"That sounds highly commendable. I don't think I would have given such advice when I was your age. I'd have taken advantage of their free living and loving. But why do you feel it necessary to give such advice?"

"These girls have been reading some of that hot literature. You probably don't know much about it, but it is hot. They think they've got to act that way. They are trying to compete with Candy."

"What do you mean?"

"There's too much bed hopping with some girls. You probably don't realize it. There's a lot of it that goes on in the dorms. Last weekend a girl came down on a date. Her guy went off somewhere without telling her. Do you know what she did?"

"No."

"She shacked up with the guy in the next room. She hardly knew him. It wasn't as though she were a nympho, although there are a few of these. She was a regular kind of girl. You know. The kind you see around."

In our conversation there was no sign of prudishness on the part of the senior. Sexual conduct, like all conduct, has to have its guide lines: its taste for the good. I do not think it is necessary to blame this on a hangover from Puritanism. The Puritans have been dead for a long time. What that senior implied is valid: girls have the right to live by their standards. That means choosing what they believe to be good. Perhaps they were left to do all the choosing in the past, and the men left free to hunt the field.

The answer to the old condemnatory authoritarian legalism is not that of sexual anarchy. In the male-female relationship emotions are touched which are deeper than the desires of the libido. These emotions are also stronger than our rationalizations.

One afternoon a handsome lad wandered into my study. He was embarrassed about coming to see me and unsure of what he should say. That was obvious from his face. He began our discussion by waffling about his theological concern.

"I'm not sure about Christianity. This thing about Jesus has me fouled up. His so-called divinity is something I cannot understand."

"What can you understand?"

"I guess I go for this God the creator angle. Creation is too complex to have happened accidentally. Universal laws suggest an intelligence capable of making laws. Whatever he is, at least he is a terrific mathematician. Someone said that. I agree."

"Sir James Jeans, I think, is the someone. Don't you think there may be a relationship between the creator and Jesus?"

"No, how could there be?"

"The New Testament suggests there is. Jesus is regarded as the Word or agent of creation. As the Word he not only created, but continues to create. When he was in the flesh in Galilee, he completed creation by initiating the new creation —the creation of spirit."

"I didn't know about that."

"Didn't you? Suppose we talk about it some other time when you can give your mind to it. You can't now."

"I know. I had to say something until I got the courage to talk about why I came. What's really bugging me is my girlfriend. She'd gone all the way with another guy before I knew her."

"You mean she had sexual intercourse?"

"Yes. I can't get it out of my mind. It bugs me like hell. I swell up inside. My heart feels tight. As though somebody was squeezing it hard. I can't think of a thing. I can't sleep. I can't study. I'll never get through math."

"Why do you feel this way? If you are so upset about her past conduct, why do you let it bother you? You don't have to keep going with her. It can't be much fun for her. She's bound to sense your condemnation."

"I know. I feel this way about her, and yet I love her. She's sweet and gentle and kind. But gee—this breaks me up. I try not to think about it. That only makes it worse."

"Aren't you being selfish?"

"How? I think she's great. I can't help feeling this way. I talk to myself about it. I thought I was broad-minded. I thought it was all right what a girl did. You know? What you do is right for yourself. But I never thought I'd feel this way. It's awful."

"You haven't answered my question. I think you are being selfish. You are thinking only of yourself, not of her. How do you think she feels?"

"I dunno. I can't think."

"Why don't you try thinking, then? And think of her. Whatever happened in the past is past. You can't have it your way. Either you respect the girl as she is, or quit. It is that simple."

"No it isn't. It isn't at all. I cannot work this out by reason."

"You have to face it that you cannot treat this girl as your ideal. She is real. If you love her, you love her as she is. Carry on this relationship if you must, but every time you start getting that feeling of the clutched heart, remember her. As she is. As you say she is, sweet, gentle, kind."

"I guess I'll have to learn to do that. But gee, it won't be easy."

And it is not easy. The emotional involvement of two young people in love is more complex than our oversimplified theories admit. Sometimes there seems to be no satisfactory way of dealing with the involvement. It becomes too complex.

Late on a Sunday evening when I was on my way to bed, the telephone rang.

"I'm worried. A friend suggested I should call you. It is about Tom, my boyfriend. At least he was my boyfriend. I've been trying to break it off. That's the trouble."

"What trouble?"

"Tom and I have been dating since high school. He thinks he can't live without me, and that I can't live without him. We kept going together when we went to college. He'd write to me every day, and phone me all the time. This past year I've been trying to slow things down. I told him we shouldn't rush things, but look around. I started going out with other boys. He heard of it. He got furious. He wrote terrible letters accusing me of being a harlot. Yet he kept saying he loved me. On Friday he arrived at my campus. I was out on a date. He looked for me all evening. He found me in a fraternity with my date. He blew up. It was terrible. He tried to fight with my date, but he was held back. We ran out and took a taxi. Next morning he came round to apologize. Promised he'd never do it again if only I would say that I'd be his. I said I couldn't and that I didn't want to see him again. That made him angry. We kept arguing all Saturday. He left early this morning. He should've been back this afternoon."

"What do you want me to do?"

"I'm afraid. He was so wild when he left that I'm scared he'll do something terrible. He said he couldn't live without me. Could you do something?"

"Give me his room number, and I shall."

"Here it is. Please call me in the morning."

I walked through the campus that was still lit by the lamps of conscientious students. The dorm was at the center. I passed through the entry and up the stairs. I knocked at the door. There was no answer. I turned the handle. It was locked. Was it from the inside, or the outside? I knocked again, and waited. Again I knocked. The sound of bone against wood seemed loud and ominous. There was a silence which permitted the creaks of the building to be heard. I knocked again. This time there was a response. It was the sound of a bed as a body changed its weight on the springs. Feet dragged along the floor. The door opened.

Tom was not surprised to see me. He blinked, took off his glasses, and rubbed his eyes. "Come in." I looked around. It was the usual untidy room. The windows were closed, and the room was stuffy with the excess of institutional heat. The lad sat down in a disturbed-looking bed.

"I didn't hear you at first. I mean I hardly heard you. My head's like a pack of cotton wool. I haven't had any sleep for two nights. I took some sleeping pills. Too many I think, but I don't care."

I did not like the sound of the sleeping pills. I decided the best thing for him was to get out of his lonely room for a while.

"When did you last eat?"

"I don't know. Maybe it was this morning. I left my girl's college then, and got back sometime this afternoon. Can't remember what I've been doing, or how I got back."

"Come with me. You can have a snack at my house."

He had on his shoes, trousers, and shirt. He put on a coat. We were soon in my sitting room, where I gave him a ham sandwich and a glass of milk. He ate and drank listlessly. He looked up.

"It's been a rough weekend. I went to see my girlfriend. I can't understand her. I've been going with her for three years. We've done everything together. She needs me as much as I need her. We can't go on without each other. She should know that, but she doesn't. Recently she's been acting funny. She's suggested that we break it up. Wants us to keep apart and not see one another for a while. I don't know what that really means. Anyway, I went up to see her and make things right. It was no good. She was with a guy—another guy. I couldn't believe it. We've been almost married. We always said we would when we graduated."

After a lengthy conversation he left. His last words were:
"I'm glad I had you to talk to. I need someone to listen to me in a personal way. I guess I'll see the psychiatrist. Maybe I need his help too."

This lad and his girl had become emotionally involved at a depth that was beyond their control. Sex was no problem. Love was.

I visited a women's college for a few days. A girl had just demonstrated the complexity of love. Her boyfriend had sold her that old line of "If you love me, you will. That will be a proof of your love."

She loved him so she did. One weekend her parents came to visit her. She stopped by in the morning to pick them up. She was standing by the car. Her lover and a girl, a college mate, came out of one of the motel rooms. His arm was round her in a possessive embrace. Someone else had demonstrated her proof of love. At the close of a miserable weekend of self-torture, guilt, fear, anxiety, hate, she tried to destroy herself. The sympathy of her family and advisers helped her to recover.

Most youngsters can handle the techniques of the sexual act. They have the freedom of contraceptives and a permissive culture. These do not introduce young people to the promised paradise. In addition, no technique is perfect when it is handled by imperfect people. Pregnancies do happen. Then what? For the girl there are three things to do: get married; have an abortion; have the baby in a home where it can be passed on for adoption. These aren't easy. Marriage is too obvious an answer, especially for parents and lawyers. I've been asked to conduct wedding services on the understanding that it is only to give the baby a name. I reckon that a baby without a father is in a worse position than one without a name. Marriage includes a father or it is not a marriage. I have found very few couples who choose marriage for convenience. They realize that marriage is more than that. I have known many, however, who have chosen marriage because they have suddenly grown up and realized that marriage is for good, for life, and for love.

"My girl just phoned," said a sophomore. "We're in trouble. She's pregnant."

"Are you sure?"

"Yes. When she missed a period and panicked, I told her to have a test. She had it. Now we know. What do we do?"

"Only you can answer that. What are your thoughts?"

"I'm not sure that I have any. That's why I came straight over here. Man, you don't do much thinking when this hits you. Give me a few leads."

"As you know, this is your problem as well as your girl's. You have to work it out with her. I cannot counsel abortion. There's marriage, or adoption."

"I can't go for that abortion stuff. Adoption? Hell no, it would be my child. Marriage? That's something I thought of as in the dim distance. I'm thinking of it. I think that's what it will be. The more I think of it the more I like it. Yes. I want to marry her."

"Are you sure? Don't, unless you mean it."

"Yes, I'm sure. This will throw Dad. He's a gungho Princetonian. I'll have to leave."

"Yes you will. That's according to the regulations at the moment. I'll phone the Dean of Students. He'll help you transfer. You can finish this term. There isn't much of it left, and be on your way without losing any time."

"Okay. We can settle that. How about Betty and her parents?"

"Phone them. You can do it now from my study."

He called Betty at college and asked her to marry him because he loved her. Then he phoned her parents. He told them he was flying out to see them and why. Perhaps the most difficult call was the one to his father. There was a rumbling at the other end. The lad kept saying, "I know, Dad, I know. This is what I have to do. I've thought of all the other things."

About a year later he came in to see me on his way from his new college. "Best thing I ever did. You never knew, but

I was on the way to becoming an alcoholic. I thought having a good time was knocking it back and screwing around. If I'd carried on I'd have been thrown out of here on my ear. I was barely making it. That business helped to straighten me out. When I came to you, I knew I had to change things. I had to do something that was right. I was beginning to catch on. I'm still catching on."

I came back to my study after a committee meeting. There was a big hunk of a fellow standing at my door. When he sat down, the chair looked tiny. He grasped a book and two notebooks in a massive paw. "O God, things are impossible. I don't know how to get out of this one. I'm in a fix, one great big fix." He nodded his head to keep time with his words.

"Whatever it is, it can't be impossible."

"It seems that way. I'm in love with this girl. I started going out with her because she's so pretty and vivacious. She's great fun. We've been sleeping together. Now she's pregnant. There's no question about it. Here's the core of the problem. I've been doing well. I've got a fellowship for a grad school. At last I know what I want. This is it. I went to go on and teach at college. But I can't do it if I'm married. I can't. She'd want too much of my time. She isn't interested in my subject. I love her. But I can't marry her. Not yet."

"Are you sure you can't?"

"I'm sure I can't go on with my studies if I marry her. But I don't want her to have an abortion. Can you understand that? That's our child. It's part of me too. That's really something. There's a bit of each of us there."

"So you expect her to have the baby on her own. How will she manage?"

"God knows. She's got no money, neither have I. She finished junior college last term. Now she's working for a magazine. She has her own flat in the city. I go there on weekends."

"Aren't you expecting too much of her?"

"Yes, I know I am. But I can't do anything else. She'd never fit into my life. We'd be unhappy. That would probably mean we'd end with a divorce. There's no point in marrying if that should happen."

I guessed that he was held in agony between his pride and his love.

"Don't you think it would help if you brought your girl to see me? It is sometimes easier to figure things out when we put all our cards on the table."

"Oh, would you? How about tonight at eight? I'll tell her to get the first bus when she's finished work."

They arrived. The girl was amazingly sweet and gentle.

"Of course I want to marry him. I love him. There's something special between us. I've known several boys. I've never loved like this. I don't want to spoil things. I know how important it is for Lex to carry on with his studies. He feels I would be a handicap. Maybe, I don't know. I'd risk that. But it's up to him. I don't want to have an abortion. Some of my friends tell me I could have one easily if I took acid."

"Acid?"

"You know, LSD! If you tell the doctor you've been taking it, he'll okay an abortion, because of the damage acid does to the chromosomes."

"I see. But you don't want that?"

"No. I want to have this baby. It means a lot to both of us. I can't bear to think of what I'll do. But . . . that's how it is."

It was obvious they both loved each other. I pointed this out to them. They agreed. When they were leaving, the young man stayed behind. "You haven't told us what to do. I gather from your questions, however, that you are sympathetic to my girl's willingness to get married. You believe it would work out?"

"Yes, I do. You have more going for you than you realize. You have a love that will grow."

"I wish I knew. I'm so unsure. There are so many things to think about."

A week later the girl came to see me. She looked frail and exhausted.

"I haven't been able to sleep. I keep thinking of what it will mean to have the baby. I don't think I can face it on my own. I'm not very capable. It takes me all my time to keep my one-room flat .tidy. My parents are abroad. I can't tell them. It is being on my own that frightens me. I'll have to have an abortion. It's awful, I know. Only God can give life. We can destroy it. I'd never thought of that before. But I cannot go on."

She was weeping softly. Life had become too big, too complex, for her to manage it. I'm against abortion. I feel the same way she did. Life is a gift. I understand her predicament. It was a real one, not answered by trite formulas.

"Getting an abortion is expensive and dangerous."

"I know. I have a friend who will help me."

"Don't do anything about it just now. When will you see Lex? This evening?"

"Yes."

"Why don't you tell him how you feel?"

"Do you think I should? Poor dear, he's worried enough. We both are. But there's no point in worrying him further."

"Sometimes things have to get worse before they are better. Tell him. He hasn't been sleeping well either. Both of you won't until you've made up your minds. I'll wager you'll have a wedding on your hands. It only takes three days to arrange it. Call me tonight to let me know. Try to make it before midnight."

At 11:30 she phoned. Her voice was happy.

I saw them again. The boy was smiling. He was convinced that they were doing the right thing. His love had deepened. It moved out of the circle of himself to include her.

Grace is active in such situations. They cannot be solved by laws. It is easy to say, "It serves them right." But that is no answer for any man. That is why the Gospel is what it is. It is good news. It is not judgment and condemnation. It is love.

That is the work of God. He wins out in hopeless situations as well as in normal ones, even when we feel that he is taking his own time about it.

Too often parents and friends destroy a relationship that is rich in potential. A mother called to say that her daughter had an abortion recently. It was done with the mother's knowledge and support because the father was so narrow in his outlook. The mother of the undergraduate had forbidden her son to have anything to do with the girl. She blamed her for her son's fall from the standards of her middle-class morality. Would I see them? Both had been so severely condemned by the boy's mother, the doctor, the priest, and the minister that they felt they were outcasts. An acute sense of guilt was being imposed upon them. The mother of the girl was the saving factor. She broke all the rules in order to prevent her daughter and her lover from being destroyed.

I saw them. They were a decent young couple. They had been caught up in an emotion and situation too difficult for them to manage.

The boy took the lead.

"My mother was mad when she heard what happened. She offered to pay for the abortion, but only on the condition that I never saw Sue again. Sue had the abortion. My mother was madder than ever. She called in her priest who told me that I was a terrible sinner. For the sake of my soul I had to break with Sue and never see her again. I said I wouldn't promise that. Mother said that she would stop paying my fees if that was the way I felt. I didn't say any more. Her verdict is that if I ever get in touch with Sue in any way, even by phone or letter, she'll make sure I have to leave the university."

"Obviously you aren't obeying her instructions. What do you do?"

"Sue's mother acts as a look-out. She tried to persuade my mother to change her mind. When she wouldn't, she arranged for us to meet so that my mother would not know."

"How do you feel about this clandestine type of meeting?"

"We don't like it. But we don't think we are all that wrong, although everyone seems to think that we are."

Sue joined in,

"Mother thought we needed some help rather than judgment. She sent us to our pastor. He's known me all my life. He was angry. He told us that we were just like all the young people today. We had no sense of responsibility. All we were interested in was our pleasures. We had sinned by having intercourse, and we had sinned much more by having the abortion. He agreed that we should not see each other. Nothing good could come of such a sinful relationship."

The boy indicated his agreement with her. "We feel that my mother, the priest, and the minister are wrong. Whatever we've done, we love each other. We've come closer to each other. We plan to marry as soon as I graduate. We'll manage somehow."

"You are lucky to have Sue's mother on your side. Do you think she could persuade Sue's father to take an interest in you? He might be sympathetic."

Sue shook her head vehemently and answered,

"No he wouldn't. That's why mother agreed that I have an abortion. He's a very cold man. He's a statistician. Everything is black and white. Emotions don't count. He'd throw us all out of the house, mother included, if he knew."

"There's not much hope there, then? Your strength lies with Sue's mother. She's right. She knows what the Gospel is all about. You feel very deeply about each other. This is what counts. Your concern is with the present and the future. Not the past. Leave that with God. You have a good life ahead of you."

As they left they commented that they had almost given up religion. Now they felt better. They realized that human problems are God's problems.

One day as I was entering the Chapel by the great west door, I had an urge to go round and enter by the southeast door. It was between classes. The McCosh quadrangle was crowded. I saw an undergraduate standing helplessly by the door. He was unshaven. He wore a navy blue sweater and blue-jeans.

"Hello, are you waiting for me?"

"Guess I am."

"Then come on in."

He sat in a chair, looking straight ahead of him in a dazed way. I waited for him to begin. At last he did after a long silence.

"I should have come to see you two years ago. But I suppose it wouldn't have done any good. I wouldn't have listened to you. Maybe I shouldn't be here now."

"But you are. Take your time."

"Oh—I can't tell you. I thought I could. It's too terrible." He hid his face in his hands and wept. "I can't tell you."

"Is it as bad as that?"

"Yes, worse than anything you can think of."

I had to think fast and depend upon intuition. "Killed someone, have you?"

"Yes, I have."

"You mean you've been involved in an abortion. Is that it?"

"Yes."

Now he began to speak more rapidly. We had made contact.

"We've been dating for three years, ever since my sopho-more year. We've been going heavy. We've been sleeping to-gether regularly. We thought everything was fine. Something went wrong somehow. She became pregnant. At first I sug-gested we should get married. She said, 'No, I can do some-thing else.' "

"What did that something else mean?"

"Abortion! We spoke to a few of our friends. They told us it was the thing to do. We could do it for six hundred dollars. We got the name of a safe doctor. We talked about it, and it seemed all right. No one would know. It would be safe. We could borrow the money, and pay it back.

"We made our arrangements. I drove her to this motel. We

checked in. She went into the room with the doctor. I waited in the car. I listened to the radio. I became worried. She was taking so long—or it may have seemed long. She came out. I could see by the motel lights that she was white, horribly white. She was walking slowly, and she was sobbing. I felt awful.

"She got into the car. I said, 'How are you, darling?' That wasn't the smartest thing to say. I could see for myself. She didn't answer. She kept quiet. Just sobbing and sobbing. I started the car and drove slowly back to her campus.

"I parked in a place I often used. I held her in my arms. She was still sobbing. I began to weep with her. We were like that for a long time. We were closer than we've ever been.

"She said, 'It was awful, awful. We've done something terribly wrong. We've taken a life.'

"I couldn't say anything. I knew what she was feeling. I felt like that too. Then she said, 'I cannot go on living. I have no right to.'

"Everything used to seem so easy. Now nothing was easy. There was nothing left for us. We agreed that we couldn't go on living. That was three nights ago. I'm to see her tonight. And we're to finish it.

"I was in my room. Suddenly I got this idea that I had to see you. I thought it wouldn't be any good, and that it wouldn't make any difference. I was pushed out of my room, and over here. I kept telling myself it was no good. I was trying to go back to my room when you spoke to me."

I was listening attentively. There seemed to be so little I could say.

"You can go on living. Both of you."

"But how? How can we? We're murderers. You cannot talk me out of that. When we sat together in the car we knew we were. We knew, inside ourselves, without saying anything about it, that life is sacred. Who were we to play around with it?"

"You can. Accept God's forgiveness."

"That's too easy. That's what we'd like to believe. How can

we? We don't believe in God. There's no forgiveness for us. We've judged ourselves, and we're condemned."

"I can understand that. We're the ones who condemn. God forgives. Perhaps I shouldn't say that: for he doesn't condemn, therefore he doesn't forgive. He loves. We need to forgive ourselves. That's sometimes the hardest thing to do. We can only do it when we accept the love."

"How can you say that? How do you know?"

What could I say? All I could say was what I knew the Gospel to be.

"I don't know very much. I believe. I believe God loves us. Jesus is the bearer of that love. We can't know love unless it is personal, unless it is in the flesh. Love is not in a vacuum, it is in a person. That is why John says, 'God is love.' See it in human terms! God loves the world. He sends his son. His son reveals that love to people who are honest enough to realize their need of love. They are the ones who accept him. The others kill him. In a way they have to. They can't accept love. To do that would be to admit their fallibility, their dependence. So he's killed because some people can condemn, but cannot love. The human side is judgment and condemnation. The divine side is love. As a Christian I see the crucifixion as the battlefield between the two. It's a conflict between human justice and divine compassion. Justice seems to win the day. The man who is love dies. He descends into hell, into the lowest depth of human experience, to the bottom of everything. That's as low as he could go. He's there for three days. He rises again: for God is the power of life. Love wins. He released it on the world. We can . . ."

"That's strange. Say that again."

"What?"

"That bit about hell?"

This is something that has bewildered me. The theological arguments I have heard for and against it have not helped me. I had found myself referring to it reluctantly, but nevertheless saying it. I had to.

"He descended into hell. You'll find it in the creeds. Some people don't like it, and want to leave it out. He descended into hell; the third day he rose again from the dead. Or, he suffered and was buried, and the third day he rose again."

"That's it. That's it exactly. I've been in hell for three days. That's where we've been. I can see something. He comes to us in our hell. Do you think that's what happened? Is that why I had to come here?"

"Perhaps it is. All I can assure you is: God loves you. You are forgiven."

"It can't be as easy as that. I have to do something."

"Yes, you can live. Life is a living out of our forgiveness."

"How?"

"Apply that how to yourself. How can you live out your forgiveness. You can, you know."

"I suppose I can begin with my girl. We'll get married. We'll share life."

"Anything else?"

"I can tell my friends not to be so flip about life."

"That's a good point. Reverence for life and worship—giving God his worth—are the same thing, I think."

"We can adopt a baby that somebody doesn't want."

"Yes, that's what I mean. That's living out forgiveness. It is the beginning of life."

"It is. I see that it is."

His appearance had changed. The heaviness had gone from his eyes. As he said good-by, he shook my hand firmly and looked into my eyes for a time. I could see into him. Into depths that are usually hidden.

He left. He left me in the silence of prayer. Metaphorically I took off my shoes. I was standing on holy ground.

I am grateful to the Bible for the guidance it has given me about sex and love. I see the body as a temple to be reverenced, and not a jail to be feared. A relationship between people is at its highest when it is one of love. What is spurred as puppy love, or first love, is something very precious. It is a glance into a deeper dimension of life. This is the dimension of the spirit.

If we analyze this experience in purely biological or physical terms, we have missed the opportunity, the moment of grace. We may respond by losing ourselves in a giddy round of physical activities and end up in a bordello type of existence. Or we may respond in love, in love that leads on to a deeper and higher understanding of ourselves and others. We may know a stone through sensory perception and rational analysis. We know another person, and ourselves, through love.

To say "I have fallen in love" is to say something very profound. Our being is in love. We exist authentically as those created in God's image. In our first love we learn that we are lovable. Someone has seen us that way. Our uniqueness has been recognized. Because we are loved, we are liberated to love. Life begins in love. This is what happened to the prodigal son in the parable. He returned home, expecting censure. But he was loved.

Love I believe to be an endless response to eternal grace. Puppy love, affection, and friendship lead to the fullest love of all, agape: the love that finds its fulfillment in the other. We love our neighbor through God, and God through our neighbor, the unseen is known in the one we see.

One lad said to me,

"I'm stronger than I've ever been. What this means is that I am closer to God. I still haven't been able to discover which church God belongs to. I think he doesn't worry about that."

"I'm glad to hear you say this. How did this come about?"

"I fell in love with this girl. We had a hard time of it for a while. We were jealous of each other. We kept wanting to use each other to please ourselves. I thought this didn't make sense. So I told her we'd better quit. We did for a bit."

"And now?"

"Now we see things differently. I realized that there was a love inside me that I was trying to keep down. I didn't let it go. I wanted my girl to love me all the time. I was jealous if

I thought she wasn't showing enough. Instead of loving, I was punishing myself. I read C. S. Lewis' *The Four Loves*. He helped me see that I had been making my own hell. Now I believe we cannot escape from God's love. I know no one can prove this, but it is enough if we understand it.

"So things are great now. That's why I'm stronger than I've ever been. God has taught me to love."

I believe that the love between a man and a woman is best fulfilled in marriage. Sex has its rightful place within the context of a loving relationship. When couples come to see me about marriage, I remind them of this. I also remind them that they do not have to get married. They can live together for as long as they please. Or they can make their situation legal by agreeing to live by the law of the land as it pertains to married life.

A Christian wedding is different. It is not a contract, but a covenant. A covenant is a personal bond made between two people in their freedom. There is the compulsion neither of society nor church. There is only the compulsion of mutual love. This love is holy. That is why the wedding is a service of worship. It is a celebration of life.

With this understanding, I realize that sexual morality may never be limited to the judgment of law. It may be learned only through the education of love. This begins with love's acceptance as a gift from God to be treasured.

6

I EXPERIENCED freedom in prison. I found that freedom is more than what popular opinion says it is. One group holds that freedom means voting for the political candidate of your choice; for another it is the opportunity to make as much money as possible with the minimum of restriction; for yet another it is doing what one pleases without thought of another.

For me freedom was an inner experience. I learned to test it with powerful and oppressive captors. When I said "No," I did it with my fists clenched by my sides, and my body tensed to receive the blows that would inevitably follow. Some of my friends had said "No" so clearly that they had been killed for it. Others carried their scars as the marks of their graduation. Freedom is a costly experience.

I received a letter from a friend I had thought to be dead. In Chungkai camp one of his men was being beaten up. He could stand it no longer. He rushed to protect him. Immediately, he was set upon by the guards. They kicked him, and struck him with their rifle butts. He was knocked out. The guards dragged him away with a red pulpy face and broken bones. I learned that he had been handed over to the much feared Kempei Tai, the Japanese military police. I presumed

98

that he could not survive their treatment. That is why I was particularly glad to hear from him.

We arranged to meet in London, near Trafalgar Square, for lunch during my next visit to England. I saw a man in a light raincoat come toward me. His face was ugly. A deep scar ran down his forehead. It twisted his left eye so that it was grotesquely lower than his right one. The nose had been flattened. The lips, however, were smiling, and smiling at me.

"Ernest! My, it's good to see you. You're a lot fatter than the last time, but I had no difficulty in recognizing you."

I looked at him again.

"Sorry, old boy, I can't say the same about you. You've changed. What a going over they must have given you."

"They sure did. But we can talk of that later."

We walked along to a small restaurant that was on the second floor of an old pub. While we ate, he told me what had happened.

"I came to in a cell behind a Kempei tai guardhouse. I was all trussed up like a turkey for the oven. For all I cared at that time I might as well have been a turkey. My head was going in and out like a concertina. My nose and lips were so swollen that I didn't know which was which. My mouth was full of broken teeth and blood. Every bone ached. I didn't think I could survive another beating up."

"Did they?"

"Yes, they did. They gave me another going over. Threw me into a slit trench, then covered it over with planks. I thought I'd had it. But as you see, I survived."

"How long were you there?"

"Over a year."

"How did you survive?"

"On very little. A bowl of rice and a can of water once a day!"

"I didn't mean that. I presumed you wouldn't be killed by kindness. What kept you going?"

"All I can say is my faith. Like you, I was beginning to believe in God. I said to him, 'So long as you're in charge, I'm all right. Wherever I am, I'm no further from you. Whatever I need, your love will supply it.' So I made myself at home. It wasn't like a holiday, but I was alive. Once a day, when I was given my ration, I got a glimpse of the sky. That was great. It gave me the color and light to live by for the next twenty-four hours. I thought to myself, you can only live one day at a time no matter where you are. I kept remembering all the conversations I'd had with my old chums. The more I remembered, the more I could remember. Here's the queer thing about it: I felt free. That's really what kept me going. I was in solitary, but I was free. I thought of all the chaps who weren't: chaps who're afraid they'll lose their job or their girlfriend; chaps who're scared of the sergeant-major; and especially those who are scared of life. I had nothing to fear. The Japs couldn't do much more to me. They could only kill me. I couldn't hate them: for God was loving me. Freedom kept me alive. That's what!"

We parted. I watched him limp away: a man bearing proudly the scars of his freedom. I turned and walked toward the Strand. As I did so, I estimated that freedom has to be learned, and that means earned. There's no short cut. The state cannot give it, neither can the university. It is something which takes place between man and God. Freedom is the experience of that encounter.

One of the presumptions of the campus is that faith is enslaving. It is presumed that a man is free whenever he overcomes his dependence upon God. There are also those who presume that it is the university which sets men free. They do not ask, "Free for what?" I am sometimes regarded as a kind of jailer, one who works to bring students into the bondage of superstition and fear.

After a public lecture by a visiting scholar from another country, I walked down the stairs from the hall in the company of several freshmen.

"How did you like the lecture?"

"Pretty good," said most of them.

One, however, said, "I don't agree with him. He's confused the issues. He's a reputable scientist, yet he had science, philosophy, and religion all mixed up. A scientist deals only with the facts, yet the lecturer referred to faith as the power which integrates all knowledge to make it relevant to man's place in the university. How can he say that? His concern is for the truth. As a scientist he can know it only scientifically. He cannot guess at it. That's what he was doing."

I turned to him; by this time we were on our own.

"I thought our lecturer was pointing out that truth is too highly complex to be known only by scientific means. It requires an involvement. Human experience is so multidimensional that no one may disregard the understanding that his trust in God makes possible."

His answer was given loudly.

"Carry on that way and we'll be back in the bondage of the Middle Ages. We have our freedom. It is a matter of investigating the evidence and making certain working conclusions as a consequence."

"Do you believe that men in the twentieth century are free?"

"Yes. At least those who are educated are. That is why they cannot believe in what you would call 'God.' They know better. In religion the man of faith represses the intellect, and accepts what his religious group tells him. To do that he humbles himself before his God. But we can no longer be humbled. We are now free. We can create meaningful goals for ourselves out of a multiplicity of choices. The goal will come of its own accord if we are faithful to the evidence."

"I'd say that we are free to be responsible to God. We are free to learn from him as we follow him. Faith, therefore, does not limit us, nor leave us in a cul-de-sac. It opens us to the truth. When I speak of God as eternal, I mean he is endless. That is, without end, eternally open, eternally possible."

"That's what you think. Faith is just the faith of our family, our peers, our teachers, and what we read. It is a stirring around of the same old soup kettle."

"Isn't that an oversimplification? Whatever we learn, we learn from others. There comes a time when we make our own decision about what we believe to be ultimately true, and live by it."

"I mean that we cannot believe in God. Yes, we make decisions, but it is not about him. It is about ourselves. We are like Sisyphus at the foot of the mountain. We are free to choose our own pebble, or burden, and roll it up the hill with our nose."

"That seems an inadequate instrument for such an inadequate occupation and for such an inadequate purpose."

"No, it isn't. We must look within and without for the means and the ends. What we find of worth for ourselves is what counts."

"Would you go so far as to say then that our freedom means choosing any stone and rolling it up any hill?"

"No, I wouldn't. It means we see things differently. Society is better than God. We've got to rid of him. What we once attributed to God, we attribute to man and judge it fearlessly. The Ten Commandments, or any commandments, were not spoken by God. They were created by men to keep other men under control. Darwin and Freud have discovered evidence that is more important for men than any pronouncement, so called, by God. Remember it was Einstein and not God who gave man the most important formula for his time: $E = mc_2$."

"The law was there before Einstein discovered it."

"That doesn't make any difference. It is man who is free to do the discovering. The universe is silent. It is man who speaks."

"That's like something from Pascal, 'If the universe were to crush him, man would still be more noble than that which killed him, because he knows that he dies and the advantage which the universe has over him, the universe knows nothing of this.'"

"Yes. It is only in man that the universe has consciousness of itself."

"I cannot get rid of God as easily as you. I can see that our judgments about the universe have to be made in human terms. In this sense, 'man is the measure of all things.' There is something to be said for a universe that can produce man, that means all kinds, including Hitler and Jesus. It is certainly quite a universe that can grant man the freedom to be a Hitler or a Jesus: you may be fifty per cent right, and I may be fifty per cent wrong. I see freedom as the gift of God. We use it by making our commitment for him or against him. Jesus is the one who has shown some of us the way."

But freedom is more than a word in an argument. It has to be lived. I have said that freedom arises out of our encounter with God. I believe that it was for this freedom that Christ set us free. I do not think freedom is in ourselves alone, unless it is the freedom of destruction. That is the evidence of history.

Neither do I think that freedom is in the law, no matter how benevolent. Law is ultimately restraint. What the New Testament calls the world, and law, are related. The world without God is alienated, estranged. It is under the bondage of sin. Law is its partner. It preserves the power of the mighty, and brings offenders to judgment. The paradox is that law is at the peak of human creation, yet it is also the means of humanity's destruction when it is regarded as ultimate. It brings men to the judgment of guilt and death. It does not bring them into the liberty of the sons of God. Faith, as response to the initiative of grace, frees us from law, and frees us for life. That is my understanding of New Testament teaching. I have verified it by experience. As I told the freshman, I am half wrong: for I am half right in testifying by faith that the power of life is not in the world, in society, nor in law. It is in the divine-human partnership.

If there are those on the campus who see the response to grace as a form of slavery, there are also those who are searching for that quality of life which is freedom in the spirit. The process of growing up is a means of grace. To grow up we must liberate ourselves from dependence upon Mom and Dad. We must also liberate ourselves from our dependence upon our teachers and our books. To grow up implies that we come to ourselves. We take our place within the universe and stand in it on our own two feet. Where is that place? With God. If it is any kind of bondage, it is the bondage of freedom.

After the death of his mother, an undergraduate came to see me regularly. He was nonreligious in his terms. He did not come to any of the services in the Chapel. Where we agreed was in our respect for freedom. He wanted to express himself freely and creatively. To do this he experimented with creative writing, film making, and plays of *avant-garde* quality. His interest was honest. It was part of his search.

He had been off for spring vacation and visited me on his return.

He relaxed in an easy chair, leaned back with his leg dangling over a chair arm. Then he lit his pipe.

"Mother left me this house in the country. I went down to check it. It's away out in the woods. Miles and miles from anywhere. It's an old house. I suppose it is a Bavarian type of design. I liked it this time in a way that I had never done before. It's simple. You might almost say it's honest. There's no pretense. It looks down into a valley and across to a mountain. I was sitting on the porch looking out at this view shortly before sunset. I felt very small and unimportant. You could say I felt the mortal chill of being alone in the universe. Anyway, I was conscious of an overwhelming barrenness. It wasn't out there in the valley and the mountain, but in myself. I was all dried up—shriveled up—inside. I stayed that way for a while. Then I asked myself, 'Is this what freedom is? Is it? A barrenness? An emptiness?' I thought about it. I understood it in two ways. First: it was a recognition that my consciousness is pointless, and my desire to be free is absurd. It is an accident, or trick, of nature that makes me aware of myself,

and then reminds me that all there is, is a moment of awareness and an infinity of darkness. It's like being a grain of sand
in the desert. I am nothing.

"Second: it is the awareness of an absence, of someone not
being there. You know the kind of feeling you have when you
are waiting for someone to arrive—like being in a waiting room
to be interviewed; or when someone has just left you. Do you
know what I mean?"

The question demanded my involvement in that kind of
experience.

"I think so. I had a favorite aunt when I was very young. I
followed her to work after her lunch one day. She saw me and
sent me back. I still followed her. She stopped, knelt down
beside me, hugged me, and told me I had to go back to my
mother. She left. I waited. She turned a corner. I was alone.
I was in a strange country. I had wandered further from my
aunt's house than I had ever done before. I was in the wilderness of an absence. I might say that it was a twentieth-century
one. There were red brick factories, and dirty gray stone tenements all around me. It was barren. I had a big hollow inside
me. My aunt had left a vacuum behind her."

He nodded in agreement.

"Yes, it was like that. I didn't accept my first conclusion. It
was the more logical, but the less likely. I have always believed,
or I think I have, that the universe is an accidental process.
I shouldn't have been disturbed by that. It was that absence
that left me disturbed. Maybe it was my mother's death that
left me feeling that way. But I think it was more than that. Do
you know what I think now?"

"No, tell me!"

"I think it was because I experienced myself. I've always
thought that freedom meant being on my own. 'I'm the mon-
arch of all I survey' sort of thing. That's probably romantic
jazz. What happened was that I realized I had turned my back
on someone. I was in the absence when I should have been in

the presence. Is this what freedom is: life apart from God, or life with God? It sure has had me wondering. I'm not so sure any more."

"How do you mean, not so sure?"

"Not so sure that freedom means being on my own, man against the universe. I did not know what 'God' means. Now I think it has the possibility of meaning."

"Freedom is between man and God. It is for me! As I see it, that means going beyond the demands of law and society. It is going the second mile when you don't have to. It is giving your last buck to someone who is as penniless as yourself. It is getting out of the shell of yourself and your environment. It is losing yourself."

"I suppose it could be something like that. That's the kind of freedom the Grand Inquisitor couldn't allow. And that's the freedom a lot of college kids are looking for. Some of them try to drop out into freedom. The problem I have to work out is: what do I do in the absence?"

"That is the question?"

This is the question which involves us in the identity crisis: who am I? One of the best ways of finding out is by testing our freedom. A sophomore indicated that he was withdrawing from the university. His advisers thought this was wrong. His grades were good, and his prospects for the future would be uncertain. He came to see me. He was an alert young man, anxious about life.

"It's so simple. I can never find out what life is all about by staying here."

"I don't know about that. You probably could. You could also prepare yourself here for whatever vocation you should choose."

"That's the point. How can I choose a vocation that will mean anything to me if I don't know what I want to do? Everybody thinks I have to be a lawyer, or a banker, or a politician, or a civil servant. I want to be myself, that's all. I could still be myself and be a banker or a bum."

"There's no argument against that. But you could still be yourself here, as much as anywhere."

"No, I don't think so. I've got to go out and test myself. Take risks. Stand on my own. Pay my way. Find new opportunities no one has ever thought of before."

"Are you sure you must do this now?"

"Yes, if I don't I'll be less inclined to do it later. I'll be processed. A sort of Princeton Charlie."

"What do your parents think?"

"I'm alone. My mother is dead. Dad is away all the time. He goes all over the place. He has a very dangerous job."

"Don't you think you are just trying to copy your Dad?"

"If I do, what's wrong with that? He's great. He knows what I'm talking about. He's always taking a risk. I think he knows what life is all about. Anyway, the only way to find out is to try it myself."

I cannot argue against him. He was saying what I've been preaching. I think men like him come closer to the heart of life than many others. They pay for it, however.

Another sophomore came in to say good-by.

"Are you sure you should leave?"

"Sure? I shouldn't have come. I was pushed here by my teachers. Where I come from, it's a poor neighborhood. None of the students at high school had ever come here. I was good at exams. School was easy, and the teachers keen, so here I came. I hadn't stopped to ask myself why."

I pointed out that his academic discipline would increase his freedom to work effectively for other people as well as for himself.

"I don't think it will help me to be a better person. I might go into a monastery, or live in the city with a fellowship group. I had a terrific experience last week."

"What was it?"

"I was in the city. Lower East Side. I had my sketch pad with me. I made drawings of people, and gave them away. I felt wonderfully free. I wanted to run through the streets.

Draw people, give the drawings away and everything else that's mine. By drawing I was seeing people. I was one of them. This is what matters."

"You sound like St. Francis. When did you start drawing?"

"I did some at school. Last year I became really interested. I'd get bored doing assignments. When I was finished I'd draw. I'd go out into the campus or down Witherspoon Street, and just draw. I'd see two youngsters playing by the curb; or an old woman in her rocking chair, on the porch; or a boy and his date walking hand in hand through one of the Gothic arches."

"May I see your drawings?"

"Of course. I always carry the pad with me. See, I did one of a guy sitting on the porch steps, just before I came in."

I saw a sketch of an undergraduate sitting on the steps by the porch beside my study. He was dreaming. His books were lying on the stone. To see him like this was to respect him. I was taken to the threshold of the man and shown that there was a whole world inside him.

The rest of the drawings were similar. Art had become the celebration of freedom.

"These are deeply religious," I said as I returned his pad. "You should be able to use your gift liturgically."

"How could I do that? Draw pictures for churches?"

"Maybe. More importantly, you could draw for the glory of God. That would be your reasonable service—that's what the word 'liturgy' means. Where you used it wouldn't matter. Help folk to see themselves in God's image."

"That would be great, wouldn't it? If I could do that, I could show a derelict in the Bowery how God sees him."

"Yes. That's what Jesus did. It's hard to see folk that way. He opened the eyes of the blind. He gave more than physical sight. He gave men the vision of love. You only see a person when you love him."

He perked up to say enthusiastically, "That's what the faith is, isn't it, when you live it? Love is like looking at people through God's eyes. That's really something. Being an artist could be a religious vocation."

"Yes, it could. I don't know the difference between religious and secular art. Some so-called religious stuff is awful because it is so insincere. It is seeing what society thinks you ought to see in a religious way. What society saw as religious and what Jesus did, were two entirely different things. The same is true today. That's why we don't know who his friends would be; or what would be religious, and what wouldn't."

"I still think I'll leave."

"If you do, go in peace!"

"Okay. I'll do that. Life's good."

One of the problems the contemporary university is obliged to consider is the problem of personal freedom. Its emphasis has been on discipline. There is nothing wrong with that. Discipline is an aspect of freedom. The discipline of mathematics or Greek or philosophy makes a person free to be a mathematician or a classicist or a philosopher. It does not necessarily make a man free as a person, however.

"I've decided to associate myself with the Chapel if that's all right with you," said a young member of the faculty.

"Of course it is. You are more than welcome."

"You may like to hear my reason?"

"Okay. What is it?"

"It's a peculiar one. A few months ago I was shocked to find that I didn't like people. And my students least of all."

"They're people too, you know. There's no need to differentiate."

"I know. You're right. But that's something we do. Shows you how crazy we become. Faculty are people, and students— well, I suppose—they're just students."

"It's a good thing you recognized what was happening. Some don't. What happened?"

"I've been too well disciplined. I enjoyed studying when I was at high school. It was no grind. It was a pleasure. It got better as I went on. Grad school was like a continuous—I don't know how to say it exactly—except that it was like a continuous party. I had to drag myself away from the lab. When I got my Ph.D. I thought I ought to slow down. But I worked harder. One experiment led to another. I published a book and a series of articles. There was a demand for more. So I found myself doing more and more. People got in the way. They'd take up time, make demands of me. I'd get angry with them, and blame them instead of myself."

"Are you married?"

"Yes."

"What does your wife think of it?"

"She's been very patient and good. Most women would have left me by this time. She understands. I'm always late. Then when I come home I'm so busy thinking of what I'm going to do tomorrow that I have no time for her. That's not much fun for her. I hate going to other people's. So she stays in. I don't know why she puts up with me."

"There isn't anyone, then, that you find time for?"

"Nope. I've only time for my lab and my work. That's when I'm happiest, I'm miserable when I'm in company."

"What do you mean by miserable?"

"Depressed, inadequate. I rate as a scholar, but not as a human being. I've got to begin learning what that means."

This need to learn how to be a human being is a pressing one on the contemporary campus. John Macmurray, of Edinburgh, once said that "universities are turning out intellectual giants but moral and personal pygmies." There's no reason why a man cannot excel in the personal as well as in the intellectual dimension.

To help do this the universities may require to scrap the testing services, keep the computers locked up in the cellar, and learn to use their freedom to live as human communities. As such they will be inefficient by IBM standards, and irrational at times by their own. But they may be free to be human and moral. Perhaps there are no means of measuring a man. We are still left with the mystery of trust. Grades can never take its place.

I was conscious of this one afternoon when I visited a junior in the infirmary. He was sick with anxiety.

"What's bothering you?" I asked him.

"I'm afraid I won't make Phi Beta Kappa my junior year."

"You're afraid of that!"

"Certainly. There are only a few elected. And I might not make it."

"You've chosen something to worry about, haven't you? You might not make it. Now I've heard everything."

"I know it sounds unusual. I've worked for it, however. At home we planned what I would do. We planned that I should make Princeton . . ."

"And you planned that you make Phi Beta Kappa junior year. Why don't you plan to stop planning so much, and start living?"

His eyes peered out of his thin worried face and through his heavy glasses at me.

"How should I do that?"

"You've got to answer that one. Maybe you could plan to do something else besides passing exams? Drop exams and take up people. Read a book for the fun of it. Argue about the great unanswerables and unexaminables."

"You're laughing at me. Maybe I have taken exams too seriously. You can't help it after a time. There are so many reinforcing factors for those who do well."

"I know. Just remember one thing, however."

"What is it?"

"Success may be your biggest failure. You may gain all the prizes . . ."

"And lose my soul?"

"Yes. Remember Dr. Faustus? Knowledge is easier to acquire than a soul."

"You make it sound dreadful."

"Do I? Maybe it is."

The breakup of family life, the crumbling of the moral foundations of society, and the cynicism of political professionals grasping for power have increased the problem for the universities. Where is freedom to be learned, and truth known? Among other things, freedom can only be learned from free men.

I learned freedom from my friends who earned it at a great price. I also learned it from my family. Apart from my father, the two men closest to me were my grandfather and my uncle. Both were square-rigged captains. I listened to them exchanging yarns. These yarns were more exciting than the ones I read in adventure books. They were about men. Men with the same name and blood as myself. I heard how my great-grandfather (is there a great missing?) was captured by the French as the captain of a privateer, and killed while escaping from prison. I heard of other relatives who not only fought the French in the days of Napoleon, but who traded with cannibals and flirted with dusky maidens.

When I was fifteen, I took time off from school to go to sea, to see what the other end of the world was like.

I was dressed in a uniform with eight brass buttons on the front of my jacket, and three round the cuff of each sleeve. I went to say my farewell to grandfather. He was in his study. His throne was a swivel chair. He sat in it like an Old Testament judge. He had a well-trimmed white beard, and smoked a curved pipe. It had an enormous bowl which was filled with Thick Black. This tobacco came in rolls. He sliced it to his satisfaction on a big brass guillotine that he had made for the purpose. He wore an old-fashioned reefer jacket. He took a puff, looked at the coals of his tobacco to say,

"So you're going to sea. I wonder why you want to do that. You should stay at school, go on to the university, and settle down."

He laughed as he said this. His blue eyes sparkled with the laughter.

"But there's no use an old sailor giving advice to a young

one. Except this: Remember who you are. If you drink anything, don't take any of that foreign muck, stick to good rum or whisky." Good whisky for him meant straight malt. "If you smoke, leave the cigarettes to the women, and take to the pipe or cigars. Here! Here's a good pipe I've never used. . . . If you have the sense to do this, you'll no need to be bothered with women."

Thus armed with my pipe and my freedom, I went off to sea, and to ports that have an international reputation for license.

It is hard for youngsters today, who do not have such models of masculinity and freedom. The so-called quest for identity may simply be the search for men who are free, and from whom freedom may be learned.

One of the most pathetic examples of this came my way in the form of a sophomore.

"I'm on academic probation. I shouldn't be. But I've no interest in my work. It doesn't seem important."

"What are you interested in, then?"

"That's hard to say. I suppose it is about being myself. Knowing who I am, and—"

"Don't you know who you are?"

"Does anyone at my age? I think things are a bit harder for me than for some. My mother divorced my father when I was a baby."

"Have you never seen him?"

"No. My mother never married again. She brought me up. I could never find out anything about him."

"Did you ever try?"

"Yes. Last year. I live in the South. That's where I went to school. One of the reasons why I was so keen to come to Princeton was because it is so near New York."

"What has that got to do with your father?"

"I thought he'd probably be in business. New York, therefore, seemed the most likely place. I got a city business directory and looked for my name. I have the same name as my

Dad. At last I found it. I went up to his office. It was in one of those big new glass buildings. The secretary asked me if I had an appointment. I told her I didn't need one: I had come to see my father. She looked surprised, but she opened the door and led me in.

"It wasn't my father!"

"It wasn't? Someone with the same name? That must have floored you."

"I could have died."

I could feel the agony of his embarrassment. His expectations were high. The son in search of his father had come home, only to find a stranger. What an anticlimax. He survived it. In his senior year he visited me. He was graduating.

"I've made it. Never thought I would. Things looked bleak those first two years."

"I'm afraid they not only looked, they were. Heard anything of your father?"

"No. I have accepted that as a closed book. Who he is I may never know. There's something I've come to tell you."

"What?"

"I'm getting married."

"Good, congratulations. Who is she?"

"Someone I met down home. I started going to church with her. Then I spent a lot of time at her home. Her father is a farmer. He and I get on well together. It is good to be part of a family like that."

"Soon you'll be head of one of your own."

"Yes, I suppose so. That'll be great. I hope I'll have a son."

"I hope you do."

As we learn freedom we learn to respect authority. By authority I do not mean dictatorship or authoritarianism. Rather, it is the freedom to be: to be creative, to be original, to be free. A person is an authority. He is an end in himself. He is the power of being over nonbeing. He is initiated by the freedom of God.

In order to teach, a university has to be an authority. It is a community with an identity, a purpose for being, and a tradition or memory to guide its development. It is free to be itself, its good and bad self. It can refuse to be an authority by divorcing itself from all that gives it character. This results either in the tragic sickness of schizophrenia, or in the construction of a monstrous machine as destructive as that put together by Frankenstein.

Protests on campus may be a rebellion against these constructions, and a rebellion for authentic authority. That "authentic" should be unnecessary, for it means the same thing. It is required to accent the freedom inherent in authority.

Our so-called alienated youth—those who use drugs, sexual permissiveness, and anger to reject society—are, perhaps, only seeking their humanity. This is the one thing missing in the age of affluence. The world has been gained at the cost of the soul. The campus, along with traditions and historical events, has been severed from the personal dimension.

Evidence of this is found in the practice of stealing. I was traveling by rail from the South of England to London. Three men in the carriage owned department stores in the East End of London. They were comparing the losses in their stores by theft. One man said that he allowed 2 per cent in his income tax for these losses. The actual figure, however, was just over 1 per cent. At that time, in Princeton the losses from the University Store—a cooperative enterprise—was 3 per cent. This was also true at Yale, and most campuses in the country. The slums of London had a lower theft rate than the ivy halls of the Ivy League. Bicycles are "borrowed"—a euphemism for stolen. Notebooks disappear. Favorite ties, racquets, and coats are "lost." Sweat shirts, sports gear, laboratory equipment, tables and chairs are suddenly no longer where they are expected to be. These are all regarded as ownerless objects, items drifting at large.

In prison camp, theft from a comrade was a violation of his freedom and a threat to his authority as a person. I remember a man who had his knapsack stolen. It contained an old spoon, an old can with a makeshift handle, a mess can, and a photograph in a silver frame. The photograph was of the man's wife. The theft broke the man's spirit. He could not go on living. The hand of his fellows was turned against him. He had lost the photograph, symbol of a happy past and a possible future.

An object belongs to the "it" classification. When it becomes a symbol, it is brought within the outreach of the personal. Its worth is given to it by the owner. To disregard this is to deny the owner's authority, his right to possess his peculiarly personal property. Most of us experience the violation of our freedom when our notebook is taken two days before an examination, or when the tiepin of a grandfather is "borrowed" just for fun. We ascribe peculiar worth to them just as we do to the flag, the motto, the mascot. Primitive men saw that such objects were *mana*, empowered by spirit. A society that rejects spirit, personality, freedom, for the sake of objects, ends up by losing the value of the objects.

We had a group on campus who designated themselves as the Seven Deadly Sinners. Whether they were seven and deadly, I do not know. Neither do I know whether they were rebelling against authority or rebelling for it. One of the things they did was to steal the university's mace, symbol of the university's power to be. It was returned, after a time, without ceremony, and without respect.

On the Sunday of the following week, a sexton telephoned from the Chapel at 7:45 A.M. to say that a water closet, without the water, had been suspended above the seventeenth-century pulpit.

"Call Grounds and Buildings to take it down."

"I doubt if they can. The door to the roof is jammed. The key was broken off when it was locked, and large nails have been hammered through it into the lintel."

"Tell them to give it a try. I'll be right up."

I looked at the john dangling like Damocles' sword, but not so elegantly, above the ancient pulpit. If it was not brought down by 11:00 A.M., I would preach under it. I did not mind it as a symbol of mortality; I objected to it as a possible experience.

All the doors to the vaults above the ceiling had been jammed. There was a hole through which a chain had hung at one time to support a canopy for loudspeakers. The Sinners had dropped a rope through the hole and pulled up the john from the floor. It was one I recognized. It had been left lying around in the grounds of a building that had been destroyed to make way for the new Woodrow Wilson School. I had wondered what would happen to it. Now I knew.

When the john had been suspended high enough to be beyond the reach of ladders, the rope was wedged and cut. The idea was that any attempt to pull it up would result in the opposite, and in the destruction of a handsome pulpit.

At 10:45 the crew from Grounds and Buildings completed their task. I preached without fear of intervention by the flying john.

To round it all off, the safe was cracked and the offering of $300 borrowed.

These events may be unrelated. The Sinners may have been using their freedom creatively rather than negatively. The feeling I had from the campus pulse, however, was negative. Its mental health was low. A number of undergraduates withdrew for health reasons. Their illness? Depression! Too many attempted suicide. One, and one recent withdrawal, succeeded.

I was conscious that the health of the campus was threatened by the destructive power of negative freedom. Just as creative acts have a basis of positive freedom, so do their opposite members have their origin in that freedom which is freedom from God. I found it difficult to initiate new dialogues or new projects. There was a cold and clammy atmosphere of "couldn't care less." Naturally, I was worried. What could I do, what should I do? Should I stay and fight? I was tempted to console myself with the thought that I had had enough of fighting. Why not withdraw to another situation? After all, Jesus had instructed his disciples to quit those villages in which there was no response to his teaching. Should not I accept that my time had come to an end so far as Princeton was concerned? The devil and the computer could have it.

At this time there was a sophomore who was making a reputation as a basketball player. He was quiet, industrious, shy. He taught Sunday School, founded the Princeton chapter of the Fellowship of Christian Athletes, and had just been elected a Chapel deacon. This man, Bill Bradley, went on to be captain of the Olympic gold medal United States basketball team in 1964. For me this is not what was significant about him. What is: that he was an ambassador of grace to the campus.

During the next two years the pulse of the campus strengthened. It did so because he was God's answer to the threat of chaotic freedom. He was a model of personal freedom, a model of humanity. The spring of his humanity was in the silent depths of his faith. I observed his influence joyfully. Whereas some of the campus leaders "politicked" their way to power, Bill Bradley continued on an even keel, responding to God's grace, humbled by its glory, and indifferent to the rewards of the process of fame.

The basement of Murray-Dodge had recently been opened as a coffeehouse night club, and named the Tiger's Paw. It was the big spring party weekend. At the tail end of the day, I was passing. To my astonishment, a crowd of students and their dates burst out of the building.

"Hi, what's going on?" I asked one of them.

"Bill Bradley was singing."

"Was he so bad that he drove you all out?"

"Oh no. I came because he was singing. I wanted my date to see and hear him. She's heard so much about him."

That left me stunned. To see him? That crowd had gone just to see him. After they had seen him, they left. And they paid for it.

Still stunned, I walked about fifty yards to the Chapel. As I entered, the pillars soared like powerful trees to meet the darkness. The organist was playing for the epilogue. About sixty couples were scattered through the seats in the nave. The music was unhurried, relaxing. The mood was serene. There was a luxury of space, a quality of freedom: freedom from control, and freedom to worship. Unnoticed, I sat for a while in the Marquand Transept. The Celtic cross on the Holy Table reflected in silver the light of the lamp in the apse. It was saying something about freedom.

7

WHAT WAS the best way to carry on a ministry to the campus as Dean of the Chapel? This was the question I asked myself when I was appointed. I knew of only one answer: I could not go it alone. My ministry could only work through the community of faith. This was the way the campus could witness to itself.

In my innocence I mentioned this to several members of the faculty who had associated with the Chapel. The response was negative, icily so. The majority opinion indicated a policy of noninvolvement and academic objectivity. Nevertheless, I suggested that we should go out of our way to welcome new faculty and students. This resulted in a walkout strike.

The denominational groups questioned the right of the university to participate in religious affairs. The mind was its concern, and the soul that of the church. The validity of my ministry was questioned. One representative from a denominations headquarters pointed out that I had no right to encourage the formation of such a community. We lived in a pluralistic society, and the university, to be realistic, had to participate in this pluralism. "That's strange," I remarked, "I thought it was my task to unite rather than divide. I got this idea from the

New Testament. You know, that one about the community of faith being a holy temple: one, not many." I was ignored. What really, really mattered was a plurality of communities.

Another church official, at the executive level, reminded me that my idea was a threat to the properly organized churches. The best thing I could do was to close down the Chapel, and not try to compete with the parish churches of Princeton.

A neat formula had been worked out in the past and appeared in the General Catalogue as part of the university's consciousness. It divided the religious body into three: the Student Christian Association which dealt with social activities and projects; the Department of Religion which pursued the phenomenon of religion intellectually; and the Chapel. This was meant, I presume, to be the body, mind, and spirit division. Such a division is fine in a catalogue, but hopeless in expression. At least it is for me. Religion is about life, all of it, or it is not religion. I have had the greatest difficulty trying to find where faith ends and works begin, or where spirit is not and matter is, or where the boundary is that marks the separation between church and society. Perhaps my vision is at fault.

I calculated that the community of faith was the only power capable of integrating the campus, which was like a general store. On one stall there was a heap of departments. On another, two bundles of administrators; one business, the other academic. On a very large one there were four piles of students; underclassmen, upperclassmen, undergraduates, and graduates. This is typical of any university.

There was also a straight line drawn through the university's heart. On one side were dorms, classrooms, professors, library, Chapel; on the other, clubs (seventeen, I think), and divided in a hierarchical fashion too complex for my innocence. I still do not understand why this division is necessary. I have been told by experts, however, that the clubs are really like life. This means that what goes on on the other side, the academic one, is not really real.

In my ignorance I sought for an answer. "It's like this," said the old grad. "These clubs prepare you for life. We're all discriminated against."

"Or some are discriminated against, and some *for*?"

"That's the same thing. As I was saying before you interrupted me so unnecessarily, we're all discriminated against. When we go for a job, the boss either hires us or he doesn't. When we ask a girl to marry us, she accepts our proposal or she rejects it. When we sit at an examination, we pass it or we fail. In business we make money or we don't. If we're in politics, we're elected or we aren't. And you, being an old soldier, should know this, when we are in battle we are killed or we aren't. It's as I say, life is discrimination. Through the selective system of "Bicker," our boys learn to discriminate in a gentlemanly way. They do it properly. It is an invaluable part of their education."

"It could be," I added in a quiet way. "I thought some who applied to Princeton were discriminated against, so they went elsewhere, but that those who were discriminated *for* were all members of one big family, a community of teachers and learners. Because they were discriminated *for*, they were all equal."

"Oh sure they are: more or less. But undergraduates, that is upperclassmen, need to get a break from their books and professors. They need to relax like gentlemen with friends who are like themselves. When you sit down to eat, you like to know who you are sitting down with. You don't sit down with anybody. Not even you! Right?"

"I see. I thought the same thing was true of the campus generally. When you are a member of a community you know, or you should get to know, those you sit down with, whether it is at a dinner or a lecture. Couldn't we live as a community of equals, and share the bread of mind, spirit, and body in common?"

"You must have been reading about Woodrow Wilson's plan of 1906. He wanted to unify the social and academic interests. He also wanted to bring undergraduates and graduates together. It wouldn't have worked. That's why it was never accepted. The people of that time knew it couldn't. You must admit things are better the way they are. The graduate college is away over there."

He pointed as though he were telling an African, who did not speak "American," where America was.

"The clubs are just on the other side of Washington Road, near at hand."

He was pleased with his analysis. It was so right, and so simple. But it did not make sense to me.

Once a year sophomores were selected by the eating clubs. A deputation visited likely sophomores to test whether they were the kind of people that gentlemen could sit down to dinner with. You could always tell when Bicker was in process. Groups from the Bicker committees, in ivy league suits and dark gray chesterfields, stalked their prey.

During the last night of one Bicker there was a violent pounding on my door, around two in the morning. Sleepily, I looked down from my window to the porch.

"Who's there?" I asked stupidly.

"I've got to see the Dean."

"Oh sure. Great to see you. I'll be down in a jiff."

There was a worried senior standing at the door. We went into the old living room and sat down.

"Let me get you a glass of milk." Off I went to the kitchen. This would give him a chance to compose himself. "Here. You're probably thirsty. You've been bickering?"

"Yes. I hate it. Absolutely hate it. We've been arguing all night in the committee. There are two men I want us to accept. One has an infirmity. The other is a quiet, studious type. They're good people. But will we accept them? Oh no! We kid ourselves that we're reasonable. We're not reasonable, we're callous. They say, so-and-so should go to a club nearer Washington Road. That way he won't have to walk so far. And so-and-so wouldn't find this the right place for him. He should go where it is quieter."

He was close to tears.

"I can't stand it. I simply can't stand it. These are not guys. That's the way we talk about them. They're human beings. It's hellish. Think of it; we can't live them. We can only see them as guys. As though they were stuffed with straw. God does, thank God he does, but we can't."

He broke down for a moment.

"O God, O God, how stupid can we be!"

Bicker, for him, was a game of shadows. It was played with guys. Those we could eat with, and those we could not.

A few weeks later, Helen and I met one of those guys with whom we could not eat.

We had twelve undergraduates for dinner, representing the four classes. The conversations switched to the clubs. "Which one did you go to?" asked Helen of the student at her side.

"I didn't. I'm one of the twenty-one who didn't make it. When Bicker ended, we were kept in a room behind one of the clubs. The idea was that we'd be kept there until we got a bid. The whole thing broke down and we were left clubless."

"How horrible! What did you do?"

"I packed my bag and went home. I intended to leave the university. Dad and Mother persuaded me to return. I'm not certain that I should have."

I was glad to be sitting down to dinner with him. So were the others.

The basic nucleus of the community I envisioned was the Chapel Deacons, a self-perpetuating group. They were excellent young men. But they were handicapped by the influence of the clubs. They were chosen from the junior and senior classes. Their selection system was modeled after that of Bicker. Most of them were from a limited set of clubs.

The campus, like every human society, was divided. It was going in different directions at the same time.

What the Chapel had to exist for was community. In prison camp I, along with many others, had experienced the grace of God. Our response to it was the creation of a vital community.

It was a visible celebration of grace. As such it was a constant witness to the eternal in our midst. As fragmented beings, we found our being in it as the community of being. We were opened to each other and to the world.

Garry Martin, a choir member, was appointed to Tunghai University in Taiwan as a teaching fellow. After he had taken up the appointment, he wrote to tell me that he had come across a Japanese who had been a guard on the Railway of Death in Thailand. His prisoners were a community of faith. They reached out like a magnet to draw him in. The Japanese and his captives spoke different languages. They didn't preach. They were theologically inarticulate. What is more, they were enemies, men at war. Few, if any, of these prisoners are alive, yet their witness continues through the enemy soldier. When he returned to Japan, he took formal instruction in the church, then went on to study theology.

The community of faith is that fellowship of human beings who are conscious of grace as God's activity. Their response continuously opens the experience to others. They witness by their being.

I had received so many "No's" to my belief in the community as the witness that I realized I would have to move slowly and patiently. More than that, I was tempted to abandon the conviction and go along with things as they are, that is, with the status quo.

Late one afternoon when I was putting on my coat to walk down to the infirmary for a visit, I was stopped by a student, a Chinese.

"I want you to baptize me, please?"

"You do, why?"

"I have been coming to Chapel. It has become my home, my Christian home."

I could not turn him away, nor tell him that the Chapel could not be his home: that his home would have to be one of the denominational congregations. I went over the service for adult baptism with him. He understood it. I then went on to say that baptism was the visible expression of the grace that brought him into God's family. Everything I said emphasized the reasonableness of his request. He had his identity in the household of faith. All he wanted was to have it notarized. I called in a group of deacons. The sacrament was performed simply at the Holy Table, the center of community.

After his graduation I received several post cards from him. All of them ended with the message, "I just want to keep you posted that I am doing well."

Shortly after this, another Chinese student made a similar request. I asked him,

"What is it that made you conscious of your place in God's family?"

"I suppose you could say it was because I realized that I am a man without a country. We fled from Shanghai as refugees to Hong Kong. From there we came as a family to this country. I wanted the U.S. to be my home. For me it was my Utopia, the country where I would be free. I read its history. I steeped myself in its literature. I came here. It is a great country, but it is not Utopia. No country is. I know that now."

"How did you come to this conclusion?"

"Many people regarded me as 'one of those strange fellows, the Chinese.' No matter how much of an American I became culturally, outwardly I would always be 'that strange fellow with the slanted eyes who is different from us.' Sometimes this difference was made very obvious. I was not expected to know how Americans felt about their history, nor to have my own feelings about China. It was as though I were being denied access to the inner life of America. So I didn't know where I belonged. I was stranded on an island."

There was no bitterness in his voice as he said this. He was reporting his experience in an objective and courteous fashion. The symbol of the castaway on an island was a telling one.

"Didn't you feel angry about this? We are supposed to be the land of the free."

"No, how could I? This country had taken me in. It helped

me to see that human life is not a matter of nationality or race. It is a matter of the spirit. One of my roommates comes to Chapel. I started coming with him. I also joined one of the discussion groups. It was within the Chapel that I was at home. My identity is here."

In saying this he was saying something very profound. Within the community of faith he was known as a human being. His roommate and friends took him into their lives. I knew what this meant. Men like Tom Rigden, Dusty Miller, Dinty Moore, Angus McGillivray and a host of others* had brought me into the fellowship of the spirit. I was accepted, the good and bad of me, without discrimination, unless it was that of the "for" kind.

This same type of experience was happening on campus, whether I liked it or not, the community was in being.

"I've had a problem," said a senior. "I thought I'd talk it over with you to see if I've got things straight."

"Let's hear."

"I've been a hard-working type. I've never been one for parties, and I've never worried about girls. I like them, but I don't get passionate about them. Every time I went home my mother asked me if I had found a girl. I'd say I hadn't. It was obvious she was worrying about me. She didn't think I was sexy enough. She had the family worrying about me too. I got the feeling that I was queer: for this was what was implied. If I wasn't dating I must be a homosexual. That made me plenty anxious, believe me."

"I believe you. But I don't see why it should unless you felt yourself drawn to the boys."

"I didn't. I wasn't drawn to anyone. But I began to worry. I kept to myself. I had been reading Ayn Rand. That do-it-yourself stuff! The more I read of it, and the more I tried to do everything myself, the more my anxiety increased. I was in a bad way. I had worried so much about being a queer that I almost talked myself into being one."

* See *Through the Valley of the Kwai.*

"How did you reverse the process?"

"After I'd been working in the library one night I stepped into the Chapel. I sat there listening to the organ. I thought about my anxiety. It seemed silly. I left at the same time as another student. We walked together to our dorm. He invited me in for a bull session. We did a lot of talking. I got warmed up and forgot all about this do-it-yourself stuff, so I told him what had been worrying me."

"How did he react?"

"He listened. Then he said, 'If you are as anxious as all that, why don't you tell someone. Tell God. He'll understand.' So I did when I went to my room. That was the first step. The next was to accept myself. I went down to the psychiatrist. He told me that he didn't think there was anything wrong with me. I'd just been worrying too much. I had created my own problem. The next thing I did was to realize I couldn't go it alone. I had to be with others who accepted me as I am. That's when I started coming here. I tumbled to it that we find life in fellowship."

In a society where we learn to make judgments about others, we are tempted to forget that the only valid judgment we can make is about ourselves, and that the one place where judgment is not passed upon us is in the community of faith. Within it we are accepted as we are, and honored for what we are in God's eyes.

A friend, who is the director of a psychiatric home, was interested in my interpretation of the community of faith. He told me of an experiment that had taken place in Germany. After the liberation of a concentration camp, a concerned psychiatrist entered and made friends with a group of inmates. He suggested that they stay together as a community. They were free to do what interested them most. The first thing they did was to climb the nearest mountain. From the mountain they hiked to the seaside. They wandered through the countryside, camping wherever it pleased them. Winter came. A philanthropist heard of them and offered his mansion. When they settled in, they kept no records, made no laws, and adhered to no schedules. They were free to serve one another in love. Within the community they found their health, their holiness, and experienced their humanity.

I believed that only the witness of this kind of community would make the church credible, and save it from absurdity. The majority of the campus saw the church as an organization that was too like the world, that is, its patterns of thought and practice were too like those of the state. Whereas the community that Jesus left behind celebrated grace, the church as it had evolved adhered to law grimly. Perhaps the institutional church of the past had tried to initiate a better society; if it had, then its failure lay in its faithfulness to the City of Caesar, and in its unfaithfulness to Christ, the initiator of community.

In a series of interviews with undergraduates I found that this criticism was constant. Not only did they reject the imitation of the state, or business empire, they rejected the concept that the church is the society of the righteous. This is the kind of society that pats itself on the back while it kicks everyone else in the bottom. It hallows the reward and punishment devices of Caesar and abhors the "greater love" of Christ.

I saw that it was not youth who were lost to the church, but the church that was lost to youth. The censorious attitude of professional Christians left them feeling cheated. What they were looking for was what the church was supposed to be, but was not, except in certain rare instances.

The fact that they were looking, and are looking, is too often forgotten. Fathers and mothers have complained to me that their sons have long hair, or beards; that they act like flower children; that they wear horrible clothes; that they listen to way-out music; that they smoke "pot." In their complaints they indicate that I should teach them the opposite. This is hard for someone of my conviction to do. I presume that Jesus had long hair and a beard; that he taught love, including love for the flowers of the field; that he wore the working clothes of a carpenter; that he encouraged offbeat music, and that he spoke of an inner consciousness that was outside the control of priests and parents.

There is a disturbing similarity between what Jesus did and what some young people are trying to do. Instead of condemning them as wrong I find that I have to listen to them. When I do, I hear the truth oftener than I do not. This is not surprising. Life is more a characteristic of youth than it is of old age.

The campus had been shocked by an incident involving the use of "pot." The forces of self-righteousness were at work. I was expected to join them. In condemnation it was pointed out that the use of drugs was a symptom of alienation. Naturally, my sympathies are for those of this classification: for alienation is one of the marks of our humanity. I knew what was wrong about smoking "grass." What was right? I learned one day!

"Have you ever thought of using 'grass' in the service?"

This question put me immediately on the defensive.

"Of course not," I snapped. The question was so unexpected that I had not looked properly at the man who asked it. He had long brown silky hair, what I take to be the kind of mustache that Byron must have had, bluejeans and a black sweater, and dark attentive eyes. Having looked at him as a man, I heard that he had something to say. I addressed him more reasonably.

"Would there be any point in thinking of it? You know what the law is?"

"Yes, I think there would. There's a religious quality which you should consider."

"What is it?"

"When someone takes a trip, he is taking it away from the world. Why? Because he wants to experience something better. He's searching for a deeper experience of life. Isn't that similar to what you do in religion?"

"It may be similar, but why use dope? Reflection is part of the religious experience. It involves not merely a trip away from the world, but an objective look at the world free of its controls."

"But think of what a trip would do for you at a service? Those big pillars, those groovy colors in the windows, and all that hip music. Gothic and 'grass' would do something for each other."

"I don't know what 'grass' would do for my sermons! Probably cause me to take a long trip from Princeton. But why do we need to combine 'grass' with Gothic?"

"Because we need to do something to help people become more conscious of themselves, and of others. Everything is so cold in church. The organist plays Bach to kids who have listened to the Beatles. The hymns are cold to those who read guys like Ginsberg. What is needed is a big experience. The only way we can get that is when we are liberated. The emotions and the mind have to be set free."

"Then, what religious services have failed to do is to increase our consciousness of the reality we know, and that which we cannot know?"

"Sure, they've tried to be intellectual about experiences we know aren't intellectual. We don't have to stick to the old forms. We can try new ones. Why not try 'grass'? My father thinks Mozart is the greatest, and we have rows because I don't think he is. But Mozart is not like the world I know. He's powdered wigs and crinolines, minuets and lorgnettes. Rock and the Twist are closer to what my generation knows."

My adviser was telling me that I had to take seriously the insights of his generation, particularly as they are related to the emotional understanding or apprehension of what we believe to be ultimately real. This is hard to do. But it must be done. New wine cannot be kept in old wineskins. Old forms need to be broken in order to set the spirit free. And we in the Church have to come up with something better than "grass."

A recent graduate wrote to ask me if I would sponsor a way-out "combo" he had formed. I replied by saying that I would.

I pointed out, however, that the date he had suggested was the day before final examinations began. The response might well be poor. He indicated that he did not mind taking a risk.

On a hot Sunday evening he came with his group. They were way-out in dress and manners. They obviously kept the barbers poor. We moved the Holy Table forward to the people while the group set up their amplifiers and loudspeakers. By the time they had finished, the East End looked like the control room of Cape Kennedy. I turned from the East End to look apprehensively down the nave. It was packed.

The drums, guitars, and electric organ were wild. The highly amplified chords rocked their way crazily round the columns and vaults. Heads and bodies kept time with the beat. It was not the kind of music I was accustomed to. It did not enhance my reputation. But it worked. The youthful congregation became a community. There was a oneness in the spirit. The wild music celebrated the mystery of grace. At the invitation to the Lord's Table there was a keen response. We ran out of bread and wine, and used water and fragments of wafers. Bearded ones and beardless ones were one. The broken body, the shed blood, the liberation of the spirit, were in action.

Hippies and preppies walked out together. The musicians, black and white, in their multicolored garments, dismantled their gear and left in a broken-down van. I bade them farewell and invited them back. As I passed the sundial, I was joined by a tall, rangy student. The lights from the McCosh halls showed me a lad with long wild curly hair, a workman's shirt, jeans, and boots. "Thank you," he said. "I'm glad you did that. I dig it. I really dig it. I'm not for religious pretty-pretty stuff, but I am for Christ. He's the one we all forget. But he's the one I can go for."

I thought this was an unusually frank confession after such a short introduction. He spoke clearly, freshly, without embarrassment.

"Yes, I can go for him. If I'm ever going to amount to anything, or do anything, it is him I have to follow. He is about life. That's what the service was saying tonight. It wasn't the greatest, but it was getting there. You are right to encourage it."

"Thank you. You are encouraging me. I am constantly reminded these days of Chist's liberation of the Temple when—"

"What are you referring to?"

"The time when Jesus made his victory march into Jerusalem. The first thing he did was to clean up the Temple, the center of communal life. He set it free. Because he did, the sick folk came in to be healed, the old folk came in to be comforted, and the kids came in to play their offbeat music. Then at the crucifixion, the holy of holies—the Temple—was opened wide to the whole world. God was in the midst of people."

"And that's where we don't look for him."

"Yes, you were right when you said that Christ is the one we all forget. To forget him is to forget his brothers, to forget his brothers is to forget God, and to forget God is to be left without a memory."

"That's quite a cycle, isn't it? I dig it. By the way, I'm registering as a conscientious objector. Will you be in your study tomorrow? I'd like to talk to you about it. 'Bye!"

I continued along Ivy Lane, past the Astro-Physics building to my home at the corner. Wild music still beat in my ears, music that cried out for a liberator and a giver of life.

That music and the quest for something better belong within the community of faith. Like them, it follows the way away from on the way to. It has no packaged answers. What it has is the experience of grace, the consciousness of grace's ultimacy, and the faith to go on in the way in which experience leads.

The faithfulness to the consciousness of grace, and the recognition that experience points beyond itself, commit the community to think and speak. I know that I may have given the impression that I show little respect for reason. If I have, it is because I am overcorrecting the faults of neoclassic theology. I cannot separate faith from reason.

Experience has shown me that this world is anything but a

garden of roses. At times it is more like a wilderness or jungle. Without grace it lacks the contrasts of light and darkness, and the dimensions of height and depth. Above all, it lacks dignity and humanity.

The undergraduate who was interested in "pot," and the one who was interested in wild music, were both touched by grace. They were looking for the eternal, or for a deeper experience of the mystery who is God. One saw the articulation of that mystery in Christ. So had I. In the jungle prison camp, I had found that Jesus was the word who expressed personally and reasonably what I had been feeling and thinking. Through him faith and reason held together. By him life was integrated. In him I see God thinking, or living, things through in the flesh. Because of him I know what being a man means, and I see what the word "God" means. Jesus has interpreted it as "Father." Because of him I understand a way away from the wilderness to the garden. There is nothing original about this symbolism. It has been used freely within the community of faith. One of its most poetic illustrators in recent times has been T. S. Eliot. The word spoken, therefore, in Jesus is the word which calls his community into being.

I understand the creeds and doctrines of the community of faith in two ways. First of all, they are an attempt to prevent the distortion of the truth that is experienced. And second, they are an attempt to put that truth into words, words of the market place, pub, and campus. They are attempts, human attempts, not divine answers. I would be a fool to live as though they were. They are necessary attempts: for the community of faith must think for itself. It has a mind of its own.

I criticize doctrines, but I do not reject them. I would be insane or, at the very least, feeble-minded to discredit the attempts to live reasonably in the world. The Communist is a Communist because he believes, thinks, and acts as one. If his thinking is not in accord with the mind of his party, he is usually liquidated. Fascists, segregationists, evolutionary humanists, agnostics, utilitarians, Buddhists, Muslims, and nihilists are in the same boat. They have a mind which is their own.

Within the community of faith, I have found not only my freedom, but my mind. Whether or not I like it, I am a marked man. I am identified. I am a man with a particular consciousness. Because I am, I have to struggle with my own attempt to speak logically in my time; and with patience, to listen to those who are doing the same whether they are professors or undergraduates. This seems reasonable enough. The uniqueness of a particular person is always expressed by a peculiar slant of thinking. To understand another, I must be willing to enter his mind, and to reverence his community truth. This, I think, is the meaning of tolerance.

The temptation of some professional religious thinkers is to abandon the community of faith and play a game with words. This is easily done, but it only proves that some people are better than others at word analysis. I invited a "radical" or "death-of-God" theologian to speak to a group of graduate students. In his address he stated that the words used by the community of faith were obsolete. A student asked him, "What words would you use for Christ, or Easter?"

The reply was: *"vital connections* and *forms of life."*

This evoked the comment: "But those could mean something quite different in a community such as ours. This has been a party weekend for the campus. *Vital connection* would mean sexual intercourse for many. *Forms of life* would mean amoeba, sparrows, or girlfriends for others. Words are only significant within the community that uses them."

The graduate student who made this comment went on to say that while he regarded himself as an agnostic, he recognized that particular communities had particular ways of speaking about the truth they upheld. Because they did, they could communicate with each other.

The spoken word is the expression of the community's thought. It is spoken and heard because speaker and hearer are of one mind and heart. I had the pleasure of entertaining for several hours the Rector-designate of the University of Geneva.

He was returning to Switzerland after touring some of the United States universities and comparing their curricula and administrations. I think he must have had too heavy a diet of methods and statistics: for we engaged in a lengthy dialogue. When he left he remarked, "What a great pleasure it is to talk with someone who knows the same language." On the face of it this was an absurd statement. He was a Swiss and I a Scot. We spoke, and heard, because we were participants in the same community of faith.

If the campus is to hear the good news which integrates its activities, gives meaning to its existence, and saves it from futility, it must come from the visible community of Christ's men. It cannot be spoken in a vacuum nor by isolated individuals. The word is spoken in and by the community. It is the means of communication, and the message.

My ministry.is more one of listening than of speaking. This is to be expected. A university is full of speech. People who know tell people who do not. Sometimes the lecturing is a one-way street. Instead of a dialogue, there emerges a monologue. In a one-way conversation, there is usually one who is dying to speak, or who may die as a person because he cannot.

Monologue is a characteristic of the person-to-person and the generation gap. Parents tell children, teachers tell pupils, professors tell students, and students study until they may start telling. But life in community is one of dialogue. It is a mutual sharing of knowledge, and not only of knowledge, but of fear, anxieties, hopes, dreams, and prayers. It is a listening and a speaking.

Some of the riots on campuses have been a cry of humanity. "Look at me, listen to me. I may be lovable or unlovable, but for God's sake take notice of my existence."

After a committee meeting where experts and elders had pinned back the ears of the novices and juniors, one undergraduate said to me,

"Everyone was saying the wrong thing. They were telling us what to do. What they told us to do is what we've been doing already. They had nothing new to say to us. Do you know why?"

"No, tell me!"

"Because no one took time to listen. If they had heard what we had to say, they wouldn't have had to shout so loud."

If the community of faith has anything to say, it can only do so when it begins by listening. The origin of speech is silence: silence, in which the word of man and of God is heard. There is more to be heard than there is to be said.

The "telling" often involves condemnation. The examination system exists to analyze how well students have heard. The verdict is usually that they have not heard well enough. Because they have not, they develop a sense of guilt and failure, or become experts in "examanship." In either case, the person as a person suffers.

The community of faith, by listening, is saved from the act of condemning. It is free to set men free. By listening it is also able to learn. It learns, among other things, what questions have to be asked. From the little I have learned I gather that these have to do with our humanity. How may we learn to overcome the barriers of division? How may we take care of each other? How may we live at peace? How may we fulfill our destiny? How may we live? Who, or whose, are we? What is man's ultimate end? The listening and the questions initiate dialogue and the honest confrontation between people.

The departments of a university naturally concentrate upon the examinables and the answerables. The community of faith, on the other hand, is free to affirm the mystery of God who calls it into being. The act by which this affirmation is made publicly is that of praise and sacrament. This is the response to God's initiate. By it, the community turns from itself to God, and through God to its society of neighbors. The community, therefore, always points beyond itself. By doing so it contributes insight and outlook to the life of the campus. It is committed to the task of seeking and demonstrating what it means to be human in time and space. Its place, therefore, is on the frontier where the cutting edge of the dawn slices into the darkness, and where God is initiating a new happening for his world and his people. It lives out the sacrament of grace.

Churchly groups have told me that I have no right to celebrate holy communion in the Chapel. I do not know what that means. I know that the climax of worship is the meal of fellowship. The invitation has been given to all men by Jesus. It is not a reward for the righteous, but a gift to the needy. In the act of common thanksgiving, the community of faith takes the bread and wine of everyday experience and places it on the Holy Table. By doing this, the community is saying, "Here, God, take what we are and have and use them for the work of Thy kingdom." God hears this prayer and returns the gifts as his gifts to us. They are renewed by divine power, the power of compassion.

By coming to the Lord's Table, the gifts are multiplied. We find ourselves because we are found by God. He gives us our identity as human beings recreated in the likeness of his Son. What is more, we find our brothers. We are one in that love which recognizes no difference between Jew and Gentile, black and white, rich and poor.

The community of faith is the creation of God. It came into being when men became men; that is, when they became conscious of their existence as "thinking reeds." It continues through Abraham to Christ: from him it will continue to its ultimate consummation in the purpose of God. My task on campus is a simple, yet not an easy, one. It is to encourage the emergence of this community; to honor it as it expresses itself in various ways; and to work that it will continue to reinforce the humanity, freedom, truth, and love of the academic society of which it is part. More and more, I am convinced that the community of faith alone may give the university what it cannot give itself; namely, the good news of God's love for each of his children. Men of faith are free to dream brave dreams, to initiate brave actions, and to point to the fulfillment of life's infinite possibilities.

8

I WAS attracted to the campus because I saw it as a situation of hope. It is the place for youth, the age when hope flourishes. True, there are some graybeards on the campus. They are there because they are required as guides, and because youth inspires them by its vitality. Their hearts are warmed by it.

There are many conscious and unconscious expressions of hope on the campus. For one thing, it is a place of opportunity. Education opens the doors of new and exciting possibilities. There are those who use the university as a steppingstone to the security of the good position in the city, but there are also those who are encouraged to extend the range of their hope to include others. Their education leads them to many fields of service.

For another thing, it is a place where hope blossoms in freedom. Now that young men are kept tied so long to the apronstrings of parents and teachers, the university has an obligation to take their freedom seriously. The umbilical cords and pedagogical reins have to be cut, and hope liberated. I know that an atmosphere of freedom may result in some absurd actions. This is to be expected: for absurdity is a quality of freedom. Along with the possibility of absurdity, however, there is the creativity of hope which reaches out to possess what is still to happen. It is expectant.

One of the most encouraging signs of our time is youth's dissatisfaction with the status quo. During my first year at Princeton I was amazed at the quietness of the student body. Everyone was so damned "nice." He fitted too neatly into his anticipated place in the social structure with a great future behind him. Now a change is happening. That polished "niceness" is on its way out. Older people find this upsetting and unsettling. I do myself at times: for there are a few old-fashioned things that I like to hold on to. But the change is happening in the right direction. It is moving forward. For me the status quo means the preservation of the wrong values, such as, stuffiness, privilege, pomp and circumstance, law opposed to freedom, and inhumanity.

The status quo can accept black folk as hereditary inferiors, hopeful youth cannot. A freshman was a counselor at a summer camp. Along with his colleagues, he was invited to a "deb" party at a "posh" club. The hostess was unaware that her blanket invitation included two black counselors. At the club, fancy with pink roses, the counselors were told to lose their black friends as quickly as possible. With the maximum of dignity and the minimum of fuss, they all left to create a party of their own elsewhere. There they were soon joined by the fair young things whom the club governors were trying to protect from the reality of life. The status quo was left with its champagne, pink roses, and empty ballroom while youth had its fun with cokes, guitars, hamburgers, and uncolored perspective. This is like an incident taken from the New Testament, and thank God, there are thousands of similar ones.

The status quo can accept the sanctity of middle-class morality, the virtue of riches, and city slums. Youth cannot. It demands righteousness, not of law, but of compassion. An undergraduate was a member of a team working in a city slum. Its task was that of cleaning, painting, and patching. The leader became angry at the seeming indifference of the people he was helping. He lashed out at them, "You slobs, turn to, and give a hand. You are living like pigs, only worse. Pigs would never stand for this."

The anger of the leader, based on law, was matched by the anger of the undergraduate, based on compassion. "Look chum, quit that! You don't need to do this. These people didn't ask you. You'll never clean up a place with paint and your idea of justice. There are worse slums than this in the swellest joints of the suburbs. It is what's inside that counts. If you can't love these people, leave them. It is people like you who've made charity a bad word."

The campus is a place where a better society should be becoming as it reaches out hopefully to attain universal brotherhood. Somewhere along the line someone got the idea that the university should be like society, and not better than it. It was a bad idea. It denied the power of hope and established the supremacy of the status quo. The campus was expected to follow and not to lead. The more faithfully it followed, the more it was rewarded by the kudos of those in power on Wall Street and Capitol Hill. In response the universities have rewarded those in power with hotter napalm, dirtier bombs, and more vicious bacteria. All of which deny the hope on which a university must exist. Student protest rallies and marches against the draft, Dow chemicals, and discrimination have been for that hope of universal brotherhood. Its song is used throughout the land, "We shall overcome someday."

My friend Lowell Thomas asked me recently what I thought was the most significant change to have taken place on campus during my years of ministry. I can answer him: hope has stirred the hearts of youth once again, and they dare to dream of universal brotherhood.

Dreaming is dangerous. It makes us sensitive, sometimes too sensitive. A conflict takes place between what is and what ought to be. Those who dream often suffer from the frustration of expectation. Hope fails in the struggle with the status quo because it is divorced from its source and centered upon the institution, the system, or the self. It falls badly because it has not soared high enough. When hope crashes, what is left?

For some, the one way left is that of withdrawal from a world which is too strong and harsh to nourish the stuff that dreams are made of. The older way of withdrawal was by means of martinis, back-seat sex, and phantasies. Now the trip from the world may be made by drugs. Soma, one of the earth gods of the ancient Hindus, has come into his own. He exchanges hope for dope. The problem of the university is to reverse the process.

Another way is that of cynicism. This is something the university reinforces because of its purely critical approach to what it chooses as reality. It is easier to attack what is than to work for what is not. The cynic is afraid to hope. He may be let down. Cynicism offers him a safe harbor or womb-tomb.

I made the mistake of visiting a senior too soon after an appendectomy. He was still in the glorious uninhibiting euphoria of postanesthesia. He looked up at me from the hospital bed.

"I know who you are. I'm not surprised you are here. For some reason, I thought of you. When you came into the ward, I was thinking what a damn funny thing it was to do that. It's this God stuff, that's what it is. I must have been scared into thinking of him. But I'm not going to be fooled. I know why you turned to him. It was because you were chicken, that's what you were. You couldn't face this fouled-up, crap-ridden world, so you ran to him. Not me! You won't catch me doing anything so stupid. I know what it's all about. It's—"

"You do. You've been assuming that I don't. Tell me?"

"It's about nothing. That's what it is. Just a big, fat, juicy, dripping hole. If there's a god, that's what he is."

"That doesn't leave very much, does it? Why, then, are you so darned angry? Why get angry about nothing?"

"Because everything is so rotten. God, what a world! The only thing I can do is to hate him for starting it."

"Well, that is something. It is better than nothing. Maybe

you can only hate him because you're afraid to love him?"

"That's the screwed-up sort of thing I might have expected you to say. You're trying to fool me into believing that things are better than they are. You are a hope merchant. That's what you are selling. You're trying to believe that this dung-heap of a world will get better, or that the good will be given an acre in heaven when they die. But I know better. Things will get worse. The politicians will screw us. The poor will get poorer. We'll get rid of those we don't want by having a war for the sake of peace. Then we'll all blow up. The last big bang will be the best bang of all. That's where your hope will take us."

"Will it? You seem just as concerned as I. There may be the last bang, but I hope not. I'd rather work for something better than sit around weeping into my small beer, waiting for the worst to happen. Don't you agree?"

"Nope. I sure don't. That way you kid yourself that things aren't as bad as they are. I used to buy that line of bull. But no more."

"Oh, what made you change your mind?"

"Just things as they are. Politicians promise peace, and then vote for war. Why? Because they're all out for power. Universities don't care. Do you know what'll happen to me?"

"Something good, I hope."

"Nothing good. I'll graduate next month. Then what? I'll be drafted. They'll give me a number and send me packing to Vietnam. You know what will happen there, don't you? I'll be blown into hamburger by a mine, or something equally as stupid."

"You may, but you may not. No one can tell you what will happen. Even the worst may be better than you think. I don't know. I hope it will be. There is more possibility of life that way than there is in despair."

"Nuts. I'll buy despair. That's the courage of accepting life for what it is."

"Even that may be the beginning of hope."

"Never. But you won't see that, will you? You've got on the colored glasses of religion."

"Maybe? I'd better leave you now and let you have some sleep. I hope I'll see you soon. If you're out before I come round again, drop in for a visit when you are better."

He never did. I hope the best happens to him.

Although cynicism denies the hopefulness of youth, it is appealing. It is bright, dry, and brittle. It is a skeleton wearing the flashy clothes of sophistication. In youth, it is sometimes amusing. In middle age, it is boring, and in old age, it is pathetic. It is the sign of the frustration of expectation, of the dreamer who was frightened by the beauty of his dreams and by the ugliness of his times.

Toward the end of the academic year, a friend on the faculty dropped in for a visit. He looked out on the McCosh quadrangle. It was dotted with precept groups lolling on the grass. The sun-warmed Gothic, and the intimate grouping of the precepts, gave an atmosphere of academic life as it ought to be—leisurely, friendly, relaxed. My friend shook his head. The sight may have reminded him of what he had once hoped for. He spoke, as though to himself.

"I've been here for over sixteen years. You'd think there would be some change in that time, wouldn't you? That is, if teaching amounted to anything. But everything's the same. What you say goes in one ear and comes back as garbled misinformation at exam times. When exams are over, what you've said is forgotten. 'They' don't change. 'They' leave here, do the same things as everyone else, and repeat all the old mistakes. I used to think that teaching was one way of improving things. Youngsters would become excited about the ideas that excited me. Some of them would go on to make a better government, a better country, a better world. But it doesn't happen. I've been wasting my time. I'd have done more if I'd joined a road gang or a sanitation squad."

He turned away from the window and sat down in a chair, clasping his hands. He hardly noticed me, for he was still gazing into the middle distances of his inner life. No comment was expected. I was a necessary ear. He continued reflecting:

"What's happened to our civilization? The university should be the initiator of the new, the originator of dynamically human values, and, I suppose, the inspirer of bold dreams. That's what I used to hope. I've stopped hoping. I'm becoming bitter. That is all there is left. There is so much to do, but nobody seems to care. What a tragedy. Hope dies in the very place where it ought to begin."

He unclasped his hands in a movement of exasperation. There was no point in telling him that he was just suffering from end-of-the-term blues. It was too easy an answer to too complex an awareness. There was suffering in the depths of his eyes. Hope had put it there.

The current expression of revolt is another symptom of hope's frustration. As a movement, it is more optimistic than I. On the one hand, it seeks the destruction of old values and the overthrowal of every establishment. Yet on the other, it is convinced that the destruction of the old will result in the sudden emergence of the new golden age.

Such a faith is too optimistic for me because it is centered upon the mystical goodness in man, essentially the revolutionary man. I do not deny this goodness. I am sure it is there. But it is not confined to those of the revolutionary persuasion. It is also in presidents, deans, and professors. They, too, are men. Once they hoped. In that hope they have worked for the well-being of the university. Some of them are frustrated. Their hope has not soared high enough. As a consequence, they have been dragged into the machinery of the academic process. The revolutionaries will find the same thing happening to them. Revolution is a fact of life. It is a characteristic of humanity. Authoritarianism-revolution-authoritarianism are the constant cycle of existence. This cycle began with man's revolt against God. Both revolutionaries and establishment are right—and wrong. What they need is a bigger hope.

The most frightening thing of all is the rejection of hope

and its frustrations, and the denial of the university's human existence. When this happens, it becomes a machine oiled by the money of the government or big business. In their laboratories and on their drawing boards, humanity is scrupulously rejected and replaced by robots. The anti-utopias of *Brave New World* and 1984 are not nightmares. They are already here.

Hope and its frustrations are infinitely better than drawing-board humanity. They are the signs of the divine-human dialogue. The Son of Man knew them well. He approached Jerusalem as its master. He looked at it and wept. No wonder! It was the city of the Israelite's hope. Hope had built it and rebuilt it. But the city had never fulfilled that hope. Jesus shared in its frustration. It had lost its humanity to the exploiters of legalism and behavioral engineering. The Temple, which should have been the source of the city's humanity, had become a cash register.

Hope died in the city and came alive in Jesus. There was a death, as we remember, but there was a resurrection. Hope that lives is not centered upon the city and its clerks, but upon God. Jesus has given us a future: one of infinitely human possibility; one which is within our obedience, but beyond our reach. It is always at fingertip distance.

The campus is forgetting this. The hope, therefore, of the community of faith is essential to the university's human existence. It can curse the machinery of state, and express the beauty of God's good news for man. It can celebrate its hope with mind and heart, conviction and joy, and organ and guitar. And it can do it through professor and poet, technician and artist, student and preacher. Hope opens the future. For me, at this stage of my experience, this means peace. This, in part, is what the future is about.

The machinery which damns man is the hope-rejecting kind of the state. It is the machinery of power over, and not for, man. History indicates how this power is used more readily for war than it is for peace. Because it is, I find myself standing with the peace-makers. There is still hope that their witness will be recognized before it is too late. That is why I disagree with some of my colleagues who advocate revolution as the opening to the future. This is just more of the same. A revolution may introduce a new machine of state, or a new university curriculum. But what is needed is a new community of being in which man may experience his being. It is this community which is our hope. Its way is that of evolution, the mills of God. As I try to participate in the life of this community, I find hope uttering its prayer within me, "Lord, make me a servant of Thy peace."

The most difficult lesson of all to learn is that we cannot go charging into the future. We walk into it patiently. We can only do this when we are willing to put it into God's hands. When we do not, we are overcome by the venom of our own bitterness. I learned this in prison camp.

I have a friend who refused to accept the humiliation of his position. He lived with such pride that the prison environment did not defeat him. With fanatical zest he dreamed up his ideal future, and acted as though he lived in it. Time fulfilled his expectation. He was free; free to be the proud soldier once again. But no one wanted a soldier of such military aggressiveness, not even the army. He became embittered. The last time I saw him he was in the prison of bitterness. He was bitter about the Japanese because they had prevented him from achieving his military ambition. He was bitter about his country because it refused to hold on to its empire by military power. He was bitter about his wife because she was losing her beauty with age. He was bitter about his children because they were not as brilliant as he thought they ought to be. He was bitter about his friends because they did not think as he did. His life is wasting away in loneliness while he dreams of the perfect war that will put everything right.

This example is the exception. Most of my comrades learned to hope for peace. On this hope their lives were based. The most gracious review of *Through the Valley of the Kwai* appeared in the *Jerusalem Post*. It was written by a man who was a refugee from Central Europe. He had found sanctuary in Australia where he worked as a journalist. At the end of the war he was given the assignment of covering the return of prisoners of war from their jungle camps. He expected them to be embittered men, longing for revenge. They were not. He was impressed by their quiet air of serenity, and by their absence of hate. He found in them a quality of hope which transcended the acceptable attitudes of contemporary society.

During a visit to London, I was staying with my brother who was ill. While I was there, he was visited by his minister. My brother had told him about me. After the usual words of introduction had been shared, the minister said,

"You'll be interested to know that I buried one of your comrades of the Railway of Death last month. You may have been in the same camp. You may even have worked together. Stranger things have happened. He was in the Sappers. After he came back, he only worked for a short time because his health was so poor. His heart and kidneys were in a very bad way, to say nothing of the rest of his body. For the last fifteen years, he had been bed-ridden. Since I came to this parish, I visited him weekly. Not to help him, but to help myself. I'd have a hard week. There would be a problem I couldn't deal with. I felt down in the dumps. When I visited him, my batteries would be recharged. He'd give me hope again. What a man! There was no bitterness in him. None. He radiated a power that was good. If we Protestants had saints, he'd be one of them. His neighborhood was vitalized by his spirit. At his funeral, the streets were crowded. As we went to the cemetery, I could see that many people were weeping, just as I was. They weren't weeping for his death, but for his life. It was beautiful. He couldn't do any of the work we associate with charity. But by his life, lived in a small room in an unfashionable part of London, he blessed people. He gave them the courage of hope. When you were with him, it was easy to believe in God."

While the minister was telling me of the Sapper, I was thinking about my embittered friend. His hope of the future was centered upon his own warring consciousness: the Sapper's, upon his confidence in God.

The community of faith has the task of pointing the way to the source of hope's fulfillment. The hope it possesses is that of working with God, cooperating in the continuous creation of his cosmos. It witnesses to the radical newness of God's action in the man Jesus. In him, hope appropriated the future. Life burst forth.

The story of Genesis depicts God as a craftsman who created the world in a series of logical steps from Sunday to Friday. On Friday evening he looked at his workmanship and was highly pleased. It was good. He then packed up his tools and went off for a holiday in some celestial Florida. That left him away out there somewhere.

Most of us have grown up with this image embedded in our unconscious mind. The New Testament picture is different. God is working, not resting. The Law said that good men had to follow God's example and rest on the Sabbath. Jesus said, "Nonsense to that," and healed on the Sabbath. When supporters of the Law attacked him, he pointed out that his Father was always on the job, and that he had to work with him as well. It was as straightforward as that.

The early community of faith carried on this emphasis and celebrated Sunday as the day of the new beginning, the eighth day of creation, the day for celebrating the radical newness of the life God had given its members. To work with God in the fellowship of love was to anticipate, and participate in, God's rule or purpose of creation.

This meant handing their lives and destiny over to God and working for the establishment of his reign of peace.

On the campus today, the community of faith has the opportunity of celebrating its hope and inspiring its colleagues to take sides with God.

Hope may release the enormous potential of the university. The knowledge in its keeping does not exist for academic adornment. It is to be used for the benefit of all people. Jesus initiated the ultimate hope of man by bringing it within his outreach. It was at hand. The evidence of it is that the hungry are fed, the sick are healed, the captives are liberated, the good news of love's triumph is declared, and life in abundance is bestowed upon mankind. Along with peace, joy, love, and trust, these are the fruits of the creative spirit. They may be beyond the reach of the state and vested interests, but they are within the obedience of hope and love.

The fruits of the spirit are reaped already in universities. Often, however, they are unnoticed. The limelight is focused upon flashes and fads. But the fruits are there in the patient and hopeful research, in the dedicated teaching, and in the eager learning of people. Greater hope will ensure greater fruits.

The laboratories on the campus, and those of the marine biologists, can develop ways of producing proteins and vitamins inexpensively and in vast quantities. The starving folk may be fed.

Much of the research in nuclear energy is directed toward the preparation of power for war. It may be redirected toward power for peace, power for production, and power for healing.

There are people imprisoned by the forces of injustice and antipersonalism. They may be liberated by the men of goodwill from the universities who will the good of men.

Too many of our international alliances have been for national security. Our economists and political philosophers may challenge the controlling powers of the Pentagon by speaking boldly for humanity. Instead of NATO, they may initiate an Atlantic Alliance for peace. The highly developed nations of the West may contribute their knowledge and wealth for the well-being of those continents which are rich in man power, but poor in gold and machinery. East and West may unite in their concern for humanity.

In the past, universities have been the schools for the privileged. They may become the schools of, and for, the people. Thereby, they may initiate the realization of universal brotherhood that hope dares to dream of. They may become the nucleus of that brotherhood we long for.

By itself, the community of faith has not the wealth, the knowledge, nor the organization to achieve the fullest expression of the Gospel. Its hopes are with the university as the servant of God, and not as the servant of the status quo. The community of faith can encourage the university to be a leader and not a follower; to stand, that is, on the frontier of life and to move ahead with it. It can inspire scholars and students to leave behind the secure and the safe and respond to the uncertainties of the ultimate. It can reinforce whatever is for the good of man, regardless of who does it. It may nurture the hope which God plants in the hearts of his people. This hope makes a good future possible.

The community of faith gives the Gospel to the university. This act of giving it is the celebration of life, and by this celebration, life is exalted. The history of the world is that life is constantly debased. God's gift is dishonored. We are all aware of what men have done to our natural resources. The fields and the forests have been wantonly destroyed. The rivers and the atmosphere have been polluted. Men, women, and children have been killed in their millions by war, slavery, and exploitation. The Bushmen, American Indians, and Eskimos have been hunted, exterminated, and discarded.

Our times are times of change. By the beginning of the next century, the world's population is likely to be doubled. Overpopulation may mean increased starvation, dictatorships, lower standards of education, and more war—even to the extent of the last blowup. But change need not be change for the worse. It may be change for the better. Inspired by the community of faith, the universities of the twentieth century may become the essential units of creative change. The grace of God in our midst, working out God's purpose, is not merely our only hope. It is the power of creativity.

At this stage, it should be clear to the nations of the world that the dynamic of life is spiritual, not material. It is not manufactured. It is given through the activity of God in the life of his faithful people. Motivated by faith, the universities may lead the nations of the world into a future of unimagined riches for all men. This, too, is a hope, yet because it is, it is a possibility.

Universities have the privilege of understanding this hope, and of working for its fulfillment. Pascal has reminded us that we are "thinking reeds." Because we are, we may contribute understanding to a universe that cannot understand itself. To think well is "the principle of morality." It is also the source of that moral revolution for mankind which God initiated by creating us in his likeness, and for fellowship.

In the wild seas of violence that characterize our times, we are in desperate need of islands of sanity, or harbors of humanity, in which the art of being human may be learned.

Often I ask myself, "What on earth are you doing here? You can split an infinitive, but not an atom. You can fuss around with the furnishings and trappings of a great building that is the symbol of a Christendom that does not exist. You can preach, and not be heard. You can take what you came into the world with, and leave."

I suppose what I can try to do is to be for God's people. My ministry, therefore, has no statistics. I do not know how many good, and how many bad, people there are. I cannot know how a campus thinks or feels, although I may indicate erroneously at times that I do: I can know people one by one. I can learn to look through Christ's eyes to see each person as the beloved of God, and beautiful with His likeness. I cannot give the formula for the ultimate, but I can share in the concern of a man about it. I cannot be right, but I can be wrong, and not have it held in judgment against me.

It was spring. The term was running down toward its end. I was writing my prayers for the Baccalaureate Service and wondering what on earth I could say that God had not heard already. A senior entered, bright, confident, happy.

"I probably won't be able to see you at Commencement, so I've come now to say 'Good-by.' Only it is not really 'Good-by.' It is 'Thank you!' "

" 'Thank you,' " I stuttered. "What can you have to thank me for?"

"A lot. I nearly flunked out, my freshman year. The switch from my high school to Princeton was almost too much. I went to the counseling service. They told me to make out a better schedule. How could I? I was working about fourteen hours a day. That made me more anxious than ever. I knew I could not make it. I was in a fix. I wanted to stay here, but I thought I'd have to go. I came to see you. You sympathized with my plight. You told me if I couldn't make it on my own, I probably could with the help of God. You helped me to relax. I accepted what you said about all things being possible with him. So here I am, graduating with high honors. Three years ago, I wouldn't have believed it. That's something, isn't it?"

Yes, it is something. There is always a little something that a man can do for another.

In the Changi prison for civilian internees at Singapore, there was a man whose friend had been sentenced to solitary confinement. He asked the question, "What can I do to help him?" The obvious answer was, "Nothing." His friend was locked up in a tiny cell in a section of the prison which was so heavily guarded that no one could get in.

One day the Methodist Bishop of Singapore saw him trying to cut another prisoner's hair.

"Hello, John. I never knew you could cut hair?"

"I can't. It is something I've never done. I'm just learning."

"Why?"

"My friend is in solitary. He is allowed to have his hair cut once a month. So I thought I'd apply for the job."

Sometime later the Bishop heard that John had been appointed as the barber for those in solitary. He asked him, "How are things working out now that you see Jim every month?"

"Oh, I'd say fair."

"You can't bring him anything, I know that. But can you speak to him?"

"No."

"Well, what can you do?"

"This is what I do. While I'm snipping away at his hair, I keep saying to him, 'Please keep your chin up, keep your chin up.' The guards think this has something to do with barbering —a shibboleth of the trade."

I know I cannot do much on the campus, but once in a while I'm able to say, "Please keep your chin up."

I had given the Baccalaureate address at a Midwestern university. It was a hot, muggy day, and I was rushing to catch a plane that might just get me back to Newark and Princeton in time for the twenty-fifth memorial service of the Class of '42. Sweat was pouring from me. It blinded my eyes. I was able to check the departure gate and rush for it. That was all. A hand slapped me on the back, and a voice exclaimed, "Hi, Dean!"

Desperately I looked around, terribly conscious of the limitations of my space-time prison. I saw a face, smiling fit to burst. It was that of a man in the fullness of life. "Remember me? I'm the guy who wrecked your sleep. Keep running. I'll run with you. You'll be glad to hear everything has turned out fine. Maria and I have two youngsters, a boy and a girl. We're happy. And I'm church treasurer."

I panted out my blessing and caught my plane as the ladder was beginning to move. From the door of the plane I turned to see him waving a brave "God-be-with-you." I dropped my bag and my robe, and returned the salutation with both arms.

Format by Ellen H. Brecher
Set in Electra
Composed and printed by York Composition Company, Inc.
Bound by The Haddon Craftsmen, Inc.
HARPER & ROW, PUBLISHERS, INCORPORATED